TRACKS, TRAILS AND SIGNS

All around us—both in the towns and in the country—there is a mass of wildlife which has learned how to keep out of the way of mankind. Tracking animals and birds without harming them can be very exciting detective work.

'With this in your pocket you should be able to interpret almost everything you will see.'

THE COUNTRYMAN

'I can't recommend it too highly for the youngster who wants to read tracks in the fields and woods, to learn the unspoken language of the birds and beasts .... it is an exciting book.'

BRITISH WEEKLY
3cde

D1420258

Tracks, Trails and Signs

Fred J. Speakman

CONSULTANT EDITOR: ANNE WOOD

CAROUSEL BOOKS
A DIVISION OF TRANSWORLD PUBLISHERS LTD

TO ANN
AND TO ALL CHILDREN
AND THOSE WHO LOVE THEM

TRACKS, TRAILS AND SIGNS
A CAROUSEL BOOK 0 552 54076 5

Originally published in Great Britain
by G. Bell and Sons Ltd.

PRINTING HISTORY
G. Bell edition published 1954
Carousel edition published 1975

This book is set in Baskerville 12/14 pt.

Carousel Books are published by Transworld Publishers Ltd.,
Cavendish House, 57–59 Uxbridge Road, Ealing, London W5 5SA

Made and printed in Great Britain by
Richard Clay (The Chaucer Press), Ltd., Bungay, Suffolk.

CONTENTS

FOREWORD AND ACKNOWLEDGEMENTS

HAPPY people are kindly people. Be happy out-of-doors, and you will behave kindly to the lives that are lived there. I hope this book will help you to be both.

Let me say a word or two about the book.

I have written of things I have known: and in the same way, the drawings are all from life, and nearly every one was drawn life-size (though some have had to be reduced). I wanted them to be simple so that children might copy them if they wished, so I drew them as simply as I could, using a school nib.

My especial thanks to Mr. A. Qvist, Superintendent of Epping Forest, and to Mr. D. Dixon of The School Nature Study Union, for their lovely pictures of 'The Deer', and 'A Young Badger'.

For all the other photographs I found the subjects. My grateful thanks for the kindness of my photographer friends.

I owe other thanks to Mr. S. H. Warren, F.G.S., for introducing me to the fascinating study of 'Flints'.

Deep thanks to my wife and friends who have helped so willingly.

Thank you, to all the children who have helped without ever knowing it.

Thanks to some who can never know. To my father. To my schoolmaster, who gave us *The Natural History of Selborne* to read.

And lastly, my gratitude to one who suggested the making of this book: Major Maxwell Knight, whose own book *The Young Field Naturalist's Guide*, was the forerunner of *Tracks, Trails and Signs*.

FRED J. SPEAKMAN

LIST OF ILLUSTRATIONS

Holly bark damaged by fallow deer. *Epping Forest. Photo J. W. Mellish.*

'Noccy', my pet bat. *Photo J. W. Mellish.*

FOOD HABITS

Feeding stump of grey squirrel (note food remains and scratchings from claws). *Photo J. W. Mellish.*

Left: Toadstool attacked by slugs.
Right: Toadstool attacked by grey squirrel. *Epping Forest. Photo J. W. Mellish.*

FOOD HABITS

Above: A quarter of the rat's store of cobnuts (found by D. Pettegree, Esq.). *Photo J. W. Mellish.*
Middle: Snail shells nibbled by voles. *Photo J. W. Mellish.*
Below: Common lizard devouring house-spider (note shreds of lizard slough). *Epping Forest. Photo E. Grainger.*

FOOD HABITS

Above: Left, Fox droppings (note 'beetle-droppings' of cubs).
Right: Dung beetles. *Epping Forest. Photo J. W. Mellish.*
Below: Remains of fox-feasts (note celluloid ring on leg). *Epping Forest. Photo J. W. Mellish.*

Above: Badger bedding bundles (Dec./Jan. '51). *Epping Forest. Photo J. W. Mellish.*
Middle: Three badger cubs below 'watching-tree'.
Below: Two frightened cubs (one gone below). *Epping Forest. Photos E. Granger.*

HOMES

Above: The fox. *Epping Forest. Photo J. W. Mellish.*
Below: 'Watching-tree' above badger earth.

SOME OF MY EPPING FOREST FRIENDS

Above: Three grass snakes 'waiting for instructions'.
Below: Grass-snake and slow-worm. *Photos S. E. Hutchinson.*

Above: Skulls from earths. *Epping Forest and Surrey. Photo J. W. Mellish.*
Below: Two friends that returned to the wild.
Left: My young sparrow-hawk.
Right: A young cuckoo. *Photos by Dr. W. Anthony.*

CHAPTER ONE

GETTING STARTED

What is the book all about?

Well, look at the pictures. Would you have known what they were, had there been no explanation? Yet they are all common objects, and the creatures that dealt with them are common too.

If you do not know the answers, never mind: not many people would, and you could find plenty of things that would puzzle me. Unless I could watch all day and all night, every day and every night, in every part of the country at once, I could not possibly know the answers to all the questions you could put.

But certain principles and facts remain true everywhere, and I do know this: that if I came to live with you, wherever you live, it would not be long before I had begun to make discoveries for myself. I should know how to begin, and that is what this book hopes to tell you.

People often say to me, 'You know, you are lucky. You live in a part of the country where there are plenty of birds and wild animals to watch. I don't think we have anything.'

I do live in a part where there is much to see—just outside London but close to Epping Forest. But often these people live in places just as full of wild life. Even in the Forest, they say, 'I'd no idea there was so much to see. I suppose it's been there all the time but I'd not seen it.'

Of course it was there: they had missed it, and they would have gone on missing it, for their minds are full of other thoughts, and they have forgotten how to look. They had not been disappointed before for they had not expected to find much.

With boys and girls it is different. They expect everything. They are busy peering and prying into everything. Life is still full of golden chance: anything may turn up at any moment. Nothing is too great or too small or even too unpleasant for a boy or girl to watch; after all it is one of the ways in which they learn. The pity is that so often girls and boys fail to understand their discoveries; they do not know enough to appreciate all it may mean when they stumble across something. Remember this: there is always somebody able and willing to help. Write to a Museum, or a Zoo, or to the Secretary of a Field Club, or to your local Natural History Society. Somebody will always be glad to help.

This book is largely to show you how to look, and then to set you on the right road to understanding something of what you see and hear.

It is not a Natural History book, if by that you think that here you will find all the answers to all your questions. You won't and, as I said, I could not write them and nor could anyone else. If they could, it would still be wrong for them to give you all the answers, for one discovery of your very own is worth to you more than a score of their's.

Besides, this book is to make you get out-of-doors, to look and smell and hear and do things for yourself. It is not a sit-at-home-and-read-indoors book. There are plenty of good books to tell you about the animals and the birds mentioned here. I want you to read them of course. It would be stupid to start to learn all about an animal or a bird right from the beginning, ignoring all that has been learnt already; the world would never progress at that rate. Read all you can, for it will form the background for your own practical work.

But when you have read all you can, remember always this. The author, unless he copied somebody else, wrote what he believed to be true—what he has actually found to be true in his own circumstances. But though it may be perfectly true that the author saw it or heard it, you may easily see or hear something quite different. Nobody else is likely to have the conditions and the precise circumstances that set the scene for you. Even the things I tell you of here, common everyday happenings as they are, you may not find just as I have told them; but you have others that I have not seen, perhaps may never see.

Yours may be an entirely new experience, or it may be that a creature has adapted itself to new circumstances, as birds and animals always do and must if they are to exist and be successful. What a chance for your note-book! Yes, I expect you to keep a note-book and I shall have something to say on that later on.

Why not buy one straight away, one you can slip into a pocket; get one with stiff covers, so that you can write and draw in it.

I've started your work already. For this book really is to get you doing things for yourself, to show you a few of the things that wait for you to begin and that you are as capable of doing as anyone else, and then to get you doing them, to put you on the trail.

But tracking and trailing, surely we can't do those in our little country? Of course we can, why not?

We know that the larger and more dangerous animals, like the wolf and the bear, have gone. They were exterminated by man so that his brother-man might live more safely. And it is unhappily true that many more of our animals, and even some we need, are harassed and hunted, some almost to the point of extinction.

But up and down the countryside live thousands and hundreds of thousands of creatures, pursuing a life just as wild in its own way as any big game, and often far harder to see and to get to know. For that very reason most people who go into the country have only the vaguest notions of the lives of even common animals.

I keep saying 'animals' in a very loose and general and a rather wrong way. We know that the living things we are likely to meet with out-of-doors, are either animal or vegetable, and generally we can tell quite easily which. Hedgehogs we know are animals, but so are the ticks and the fleas that infest them. Birds are animals, and so are the lice that live in their feathers. Snails, slugs and centipedes are animals, and so are flies and worms. But in this book we shall speak of Birds as birds, and when we say 'animals', we are thinking only of those with backbones, the Vertebrates. And even then we shall miss out the Fish, so that by animals we mean, Amphibians, Reptiles and Mammals.

I want you to try, as we go on, to capture some of the joy and the thrill of learning of these animals for yourself, to feel the joy of 'following the trail'; the entertainment and the understanding that are to be yours if you take up the art of tracking. The excitement too; the thrill of the hunter come not to kill, but to watch and to learn, to watch creatures that have learnt to keep out of man's way, out of his sight—creatures with nose and ears and eyes many times sharper than your own.

It need cost you nothing, it kills nothing, it robs nothing and it takes nothing but patience and time. You will never come to the end of it; no one has ever learnt all there is to learn about any wild creature, for each individual is different from every other. That is character, which wild animals possess, just as you are different in so many little ways from every other human being.

There was a time, not so distant as history goes, when the people in these islands knew the signs of the trail as we never shall. They needed to; their living, often their very life, depended on it. They were always following the trail. Not just a trail of footprints; animals have to use more of their bodies than just their feet. The dropped feather, the feather caught on a bush, the scattered feathers from a kill, the bitten grass, the hole in the earth, the claw-mark in the bark of a tree, the teeth-marks in a wasted fruit, torn-out fur, droppings, the cries of bird and animal; they all were read just as you read this book. And far more so, for the hunter read more into them.

A hoofmark was not just a hoofmark, not even a hoof-mark of one particular animal. It had character, it had age. Its character depended partly on the nature of the ground. Then the print could tell the sex of the animal, whether it was male or female; it gave away the maker's age; it told, or it began to tell, the condition of the animal at the time, whether it was ill or well, lame or fit. It told what it was doing, or trying to do; it showed plainly the state of the ground at the time and the weather since, and how long had passed since its making.

All that from one footprint?

Yes, many people in the world today could still do it. And they could do it as well as our forebears did, before civilisation came and made us forget that we were born blessed with sight and hearing, and the sense of taste and smell and touch.

What have your senses taught you, of our wild animals? Do you remember I said there were thousands of them up and down the countryside, almost unknown, waiting for you to discover them? Test yourself. What do you know of the life-story of a weasel or of a field-mouse, or even of the common vole that teems in our pastures and rough wastes?

Plenty to learn, isn't there? Fascinating stories to unravel, and perhaps the chance of a real discovery. You may add something to the store of knowledge in the world. Without looking for it even, you may be given some new and vital piece of information, something that nobody else has ever seen or heard.

Even if you do not add to the world's store of knowledge, you will certainly add to your own and to your enjoyment. Instead of going to the country and finding it rather a dull place with very few cinemas and nowhere to go—yes, I've known people say that!—you will find it a place simply full of life and interest and exciting things to do.

But how are you to know that all these animals are really there, when you do not see them?

Just sit a moment quietly, and think. Try to remember all the animals you have seen or heard of, killed upon the roads. I cannot know what you are thinking, so here is my list: Rabbits, hedgehogs, stoats, squirrels, mice, rats, voles, moles, shrews, foxes, badgers, deer, grass-snakes, lizards, frogs, toads, newts, little owls, barn owls, thrushes, blackbirds, chaffinches, sparrows, crows, moorhens, yellowhammers. And so I could go on. I suppose it is true to say that at some time or other, practically every species of wild animal we possess has been found dead upon the roads—and many, many birds.

After all, it is not surprising. We kill and injure upon those same roads thousands of human beings every year. These unhappy people were caught although they knew all about roads. How can we expect the wild animals to escape?

It is true of course that animals and birds get used to roads, and the population in hedge and bank along a main road may actually be far higher than in a lonely field. Yet, on the other hand, we have all these dead creatures.

Why? Why were they there at all? What sort of individual could they have been? Just supremely unlucky? Or were they ill? Were they old and slow, or young and inexperienced? Some are fully grown; many are young, in the first few months of life. What were they doing on the roads? Had mother—or father—turned them out to fend for themselves and they were seeking new homes? Or were they looking for hibernating quarters? Many, certainly, of the older animals were. Here is something worth thinking about. You might begin a study of it.

And what about the spring slaughter of newts, and toads and frogs? Yes, I thought you'd know the answer to that. They are amphibians, creatures that live two lives, first as 'fish', breathing air from the water, and then as land creatures. These, now land animals, were off to the ponds to breed, following an inborn urge that sends them to water that their offspring may be born in the right environment. And here they are, squashed on the roads.

It is all very unpleasant, this talk of killing and of dead things, especially when we want to find the live ones.

But it proves something. It proves the animals are still there. Not only were there but are there. For those killed are but a fraction of the wild population of these islands.

The animals are there; not only in the country but around the towns, and even in the very towns themselves. Yes, here at home, under your very eyes and nose, live all kinds of creatures you never see—they take good care of that—and whose presence therefore you do not suspect.

Rabbits, dozens of them, live in built-up areas, wherever there's a stretch of grass, and bank-and-hedge or a thicket, or a raised sports pavilion, to give them cover. Scarcely ever is one of these rabbits caught. All the dogs in the neighbourhood know them and hunt them with gusto. But the rabbits know all about dogs, and all that they need to know of the human beings the dogs bring with them.

There are hedgehogs in many gardens within town boundaries. They have been there generation after generation, scarcely ever seen, unless someone finds one by accident or puts out food to attract them.

Then there are mice and voles and rats; hundreds of rats, whole colonies of them, living dangerously, right in the very work-places and play-places of us all. They kill and eat the young birds. They destroy our food; they eat the remains of picnic lunches and the bait left by the fisherman on the bank. They dwell under the plank that makes a bridge across the stream; they even have fortresses under the very duckboards of landing-stages, where people stamp and dogs run and sniff all day.

Farther afield, and not so far, are badgers and foxes and otters, and stoats and weasels and squirrels, all to be watched, and watched easily if you know how.

The world is full of life; our islands no less than other lands. The wild creatures have fitted themselves into man's changing countryside, each animal in its own territory, sufficient for its own needs. They are there, the animals, and now your task is to know how to set about finding them.

CHAPTER TWO

THINKING IT OUT FIRST

I feel proud when I think of writing this chapter. Not proud of anything that I have done, but of all those people in this country and abroad, who have helped me. People who have never been too tired to say 'Come, and welcome,' instead of 'Oh, I can't be bothered today, can't you make it some other time?' People who have never said 'Why don't you find out for yourself instead of picking my brains?'

The answer to that, of course, would be that you cannot possibly be everywhere at once and see and hear everything. Your own eyes and ears must be your friends if you are going to get the fullest enjoyment out of your life, to get the zest out of living, but after that you are going to depend time and again on the knowledge and the kindness of other people.

What sort of people? I shall tell you of some, but then I must add 'Almost anybody'. You never know who is going to be interested or in what their interest will lie. People in all branches of life are specialists in some aspect or other of natural history, and usually they are only too happy to share their interest and their knowledge.

I can never thank enough those who have given of their time and patience and experience to further my knowledge and my pleasure. Professors, scientists, a voice in a wireless programme, an author speaking through his book, farmers and farm labourers, land-owners and their gamekeepers, those quiet enthusiasts who work in museums, officials and the staff of the Metropolitan Water Board, Directors of Zoos, and Zoo Keepers. And the Keepers of Epping Forest, who in their busy days have found time to help me in so many ways, and so cheerfully.

You might start by making friends with a Keeper. If there is a wood of any size near your home, find out who the Keeper is, and get to know him. He will show you how to find the birds and the mammals, and how to watch without being seen, or at least without scaring away what it is you are watching. He can teach you how to handle animals without frightening or hurting them. Watch his dog, and then ask yourself if yours is as well-trained; and if not, why not?

Then there are the woodsmen who live most of their lives with trees, and understand and feel for them as possibly nobody else can. They too know the wild life of the woods with an intimate knowledge that comes from years of being friends to almost every living thing.

Talk with these men who have, so many of them, what a friend of mine calls 'the soft woodman's voice'. Their ears are attuned to the sounds of wood and forest. They have no craving for wireless blaring all day long. To them the harsh and strident noises of our modern world are out of tune with life, and painful.

But because I tell you of all these people, and I would add the many folk who have asked me in to share some happy secret hidden in their own garden, I would not have you think that life in the country is all holiday. People who work on the land are as fully occupied as anyone. They may not be rushing about, tearing their nervous systems to pieces, as we in towns so often do. But they are just as busy, and their work is highly skilled and hard. Because you are on holiday it does not mean that everybody else is on holiday too. Indeed, for those whose living depends on the land, your holiday may well come in their busiest season and you are just in the way. The wonder is that we are made so welcome.

Here is another fact we might do well to remember —and it is one forgotten by many—that in every square yard of land in these islands somebody has an interest. It is true you may walk for miles unhindered; but really you go on sufferance, because you are allowed to do so as long as you behave. This is even more true where land is precious and must be used for cattle and for crops. It doesn't mean that someone is watching you all the time to see what mischief you are up to. You are taken on trust, and the farmer or landowner who lets you wander through his fields depends on you to look after them, just as he would be careful if he came into your garden. He is far too busy, even if he wanted to do it, to keep an eye on all his visitors. All the same you would be surprised how far and how much he can see in those fields that he knows better than you know your own road or street. The sound of a voice, a glimpse of a head or a shirt through the hedge, and he has a pretty shrewd idea of what is taking place. Remember that he takes you on trust and would far rather not be let down. If you are really interested in the subject of this book, you will see that you keep your farmer friends, and you will never regret it.

But if people own the land, and they are all too busy

to be out and about with you, then who is going to help you? Probably those very ones; busy people are usually the ones who find time for a little extra work. Many landowners indeed are keen naturalists and only too happy to help others.

We have spoken of the people whose daily life takes them into woods and fields all day and every day, and often by night too.

There are others. You may find one in every village, I suppose, throughout the world. People who just cannot keep away from the fields, born with a longing to be out-of-doors, and never so happy as when they are alone. Get to know one if you can, though it may take you a long time. He may not want you with him. He may say little of what he does when he is alone. But persevere, and if your friendship is sincere he will soon see that you are not merely a nuisance who asks questions without really wanting the answer. Then, when you are accepted, you will find that he has lived more closely to the life of the birds and the wild creatures than anyone you have met before. These people are born with the listening ear, the attentive eye, the patience of understanding. They can stand or sit for hours watching happily—'wasting time', if you like, and certainly some would call it that. But let us not be hasty in our judgment. For all the time they are learning what they want to learn; they are tranquil and happy-minded; they are filled with a deep sense of satisfaction in life, and we should all be better for having that.

They see and hear the things that cannot be put into museums and that seldom appear in books.

But how are you going to find these people?

I think they will find you. They will probably know of you long before they let you know them. But if you go out-of-doors, not with stick or catapult but with a desire for friendship, they will certainly find you. They will know much of you; they will have watched your actions and judged on what they have seen. If they can feel that you have that something which they themselves possess—a something which is largely a love of the countryside and makes you at peace in the country and, even more, puts the countryside at peace with you, then you will find your friends without seeking them. They will gather round you and, whenever there is something you should see or hear, a quiet word will let you know.

Is this just airy talk? I know it isn't, for I have these friends myself. Some I found by chance, and only chance can ever bring us together again, but we are friends. A word spoken here, a bird watched in flight there, a sunset spoken of by a man with the hands of a navvy and the heart of a poet, and I have found a new friend, one who asks nothing through the years but to keep his friendship, and the chance to speak again of the things he loves.

And now, after saying all this, you may think it strange that the next part of the chapter deals not with what you can find out-of-doors but with maps. But, after all, they are to get you out-of-doors. It wouldn't be fair to expect to be told everything, even the way about. Where would be your joy as a discoverer if someone else has to do all the exploring for you? The study of maps is fascinating, but that is a subject you can read of elsewhere.

All I want to begin with is that you shall use your

map to learn the general lie of the land. Make a simple copy of it for yourself, putting in the main roads and woods and any rivers or lakes. Learn by heart the way to your chosen spot; be able to close your eyes and see the path to it. Once you have learned a way for yourself you can never forget it. Do not be like the girls and boys who have asked me to tell them where to go and how to get there—and—could I go with them? As a rule, I cannot. Their lives have not yet reached the busy stage; mine has. But even if I could go, why should I, and rob them of the thrill of discovery? 'Buy a map,' I advise them, 'and I'll show you how to start using it, and then the rest is up to you.'

We begin by learning the main roads and their direction. With those fixed in your memory you can never be really lost. For main roads are easily found, and any passer will be able to help you. The map itself will help you to find them. To begin with it gives their direction, for maps are printed so that the top, unless it says otherwise, is North. Top, North; right, East; left, West; perfectly simple but of the greatest help in planning your route.

To know that as you travel you have only to bear in mind the hour and the whereabouts of the sun, or the direction of the day's wind, or the lie of the main road that you can follow by the telephone posts, or of the distant railway betrayed by the smoke of engines, to keep yourself on the map and on your walk. Later, you will find other things on your map that will help you to know your whereabouts.

It marks the church on the hill and tells what kind of church building it is. It gives the sites of inns and of public houses. It shows the post office telephone (a use-

23

ful thing to know), the power cables, windmills, the windpumps. Learn the symbols for these, and put them on your own map as you discover them on your walks. It will improve your local geography and will be training your powers of observation.

Have another look at your map. Do you see thin lines with numbers—lines that enclose regularly less and less space as the numbers get bigger? These are 'contours', and they are a picture of what you would see if you could draw lines at the same levels round the hills and then look down upon them from above. The numbers give the heights above sea-level, and the space they enclose is the top of the hill.

Contours are worth your study. They show the peaks that can be seen from a given point, and why others are hidden. They show you valleys before you ever see them, so that you know whether the stream meanders peacefully or rushes down as a mountain torrent. They show the great roll of hills and the breath-taking steepness of an escarpment where the hill falls suddenly away.

Learn to read your map as you would a book. When you read, your eye travels ahead of what your brain is saying. So you should read a map not merely to say 'Now, where am I—let me have a look at the map!' Be able to see from the map what lies ahead of you, what you may expect in the way of scenery.

I remember my wife and I toiling with our packs, up a steep hill road in the Yorkshire Dales.

'Never mind,' I said, 'just where we turn to the right at the top, there'll be a splendid view.' At the very top the road swept right, but there was no view; a fringe of lofty trees hid everything. So we pushed through and there it was, the whole Dale—a dale or vale, is a valley—peaceful and contented in the sun, stone walls around the hill farms, trees close-clustered for shelter against the winds, the village far away, and the white road running through. Yet, if we had not read our maps, we might have seen nothing of it.

One thing more about maps, and one you can learn how to use from the map itself. You may find the whole of your map divided into squares with numbers at the ends of the lines. These are the grid numbers, and the lines are grid lines. Later you will find them of the greatest use in making notes to remember places of especial interest. The use of the grid is simplicity itself, so learn to use it.

And now, take care of your map. I dislike to see them tattered and frayed and dirtied. When I can, I buy a dissected map, that is one cut up into pocket-sized lozenges and remounted on linen, with sufficient space between the lozenges to allow for folding. If you cannot get a dissected map, at least you can slip yours into a transparent cover; and remember to write your name and address clearly on the blank back of the map. It will not guarantee the return of a lost map (at least it hasn't mine) but you will have done your best. A well-used map becomes a well-loved friend; and no one likes to lose a friend.

And now, let us suppose that you have found your way about on the map, and you know where you want to go to start your 'tracking and trailing'. I can have no idea of that, even of the kind of locality you have chosen. But I can say this; that if you have bought a good map and if you have studied it well, then you will have some idea of what to expect, even before you set out.

You have chosen, we will say, a wood on a hill—just the place you might well choose. Before ever you see it you should have a rough idea of its possibilities.

You will know from your general knowledge of local geography whether it is on chalk or clay, in limestone country or on sand; and that will make a difference to the wood itself.

Then, from the contour lines, you can learn its height above sea-level, and in which direction it is most exposed, and what protection it is likely to have from prevailing winds. You will see the streams and read their nature from the map.

The soil, we said, affects the nature of the wood; it has indeed enormous effect upon its vegetation. If you do not know the trees and shrubs, then make up your mind that you are going to learn them, a new one if possible at each visit, for you are never going to be able to follow your work successfully if the common trees and bushes—and their fruits—are strangers to you. They are food and home for the animals and the birds you hope to study—so they are nearly as important for you as for them.

In imagination now draw near to your wood. Up the slope ahead stands its bulk, friendly and comfortable against the sky and full of you know not what surprises.

And there's the first surprise—barbed wire, running round the lower fringe. Well, is that all? Or is barbed wire worthy of a closer look? Surely animals leave telltale traces on barbs; pieces of coat torn out as they squeezed under, or pulled as they brushed by? Horse and cow and sheep, deer and fox and badger, may all leave the snatch of hair that betrays them. Barbed wire is indeed worth looking at with a keen eye.

Beyond the wire, leading into the thickets of bramble and brier, are little tunnels; they deserve examination for themselves; and they too have hairs dropped and lying loose or trodden into the run, or caught up on twigs or thorns on the sides or roof of the tunnel. There, too, where the grass ends and the floor is of earth, are footprints.

Tunnels lead, naturally enough, to holes—holes in the ground. Think of our wild animals, and it may surprise you to realise how many of them live at least part of their lives underground. Badger, fox, otter, stoat and weasel, vole, mole, rabbit, these are the commoner ones. Not all holes are in the ground. They may be under logs or at the base of trees, or in the tree trunk itself—but I shall speak of holes again in a later chapter.

In the wood will be nests. The squirrel's drey which may house the rare and lovely marten; the nests of crow and jay and magpie and of the smaller birds they rob; little domed nests in the grass under the bramble edge, of willow wren; nests of grass like cups, of lark and pipit. Giant nests of twigs like the buzzard's; great nests of heron; the bottle-nest of the long-tailed tit, fragile yet strong, and most beautiful. Nests there will be everywhere, despite all the robbing by bird and boy.

And you may easily find them with a little looking. The splash on the trunk below a starling hole, the worn and lighter-coloured bark around the woodpeckers' nest, the wood chippings on the ground where they have been excavating, the splash of yellow where the owl sat before flying off into the dusk, the tiny splashes in a bush where a nest is hidden, the wisp of feather or of grass caught in the roughness of the bark near a nest hole; any and all may betray the home that is in use. Use your eyes, and remember that just because you have missed them on your first visit, it doesn't in the least mean that your wood is 'empty'. You will discover something new at every coming.

And even without finding their homes there is much work you can do to help you to understand the animals. There will be the remains of feastings since bird and animal must eat to live, and since most are 'opportunity feeders'—feeding well whenever they come upon the chance. There must be droppings too, since no animal can remain in health and still have inside it all the waste and unwanted food material. Food tracks; droppings; I want you to bear them both in mind. You may not think them very savoury subjects for investigation and discussion, but long before you have become an accomplished tracker you will find them of the liveliest interest.

While you are looking for food tracks and for droppings, you will certainly find feathers; and nobody can feel anything but pleasure at finding so lovely a thing. Feathers will tell you more of the tale of the woods, of its inhabitants, and of its visitors.

A fallen feather may tell a bird is moulting, like the exquisite wing covert feathers of the jay that we may find in June and July, blue and black and white. In the winter are pigeon feathers; the white-banded dark tail feathers, the stiff wing primary that cleaves the air with swift flight, the little downy feathers that kept the body warm. The down lies like flakes of snow when the pigeon flocks are in the oak and beech woods. In the trees the birds sit, facing wind, and preen before they sleep, and the dawn finds the feather-flakes on the brown floor. When they fly there are feathers again, caught on the stems of bushes. Some will be in silver birch. Feel the stems of the birches; some are downy smooth, and others rough with tiny white coruscations. See in which the feathers hang; and you will learn of both bird and bush. Little points such as this can make the day rich with added interest; and the more you observe the more will come to your notice, till every moment reveals some secret and its cause.

Go in September, when the sun is shining on your hill and only the wood is shrouded with late mist. See how the sunbeams falling through the mist have warmed the earth below, and how the warm air rising has strength to move leaves and slender branches of the trees above, while all the wood beside stands without stirring.

Or come into the winter wood when the leaves are crisp-edged with frost, and see, as I have seen, the scatterings of twenty-four pigeons in twelve weeks— feathers plucked by the sparrow-hawk that snatched the pigeon from the flock. There, yards away, is the tiny handful of feathers where the bird was struck and the feathers drifted from it. Come upon the hawk at his work, and he leaves his plucking and goes, but only to return and find the bird again, though you have moved it yards away. Examine it before he comes and you will see where the beak bit through into his victim's brain, the first morsel to be eaten.

Come again in the late spring when all the woods are green and the young hawks are wheezing their hunger from the nest twenty feet above your head, and you will find between the bushes the tragic little scatterings of robin and titmouse, killed to feed the young.

Feathers and tunnels, holes and hair, what else might you expect to see?

Runs in the grass; the little lanes that rabbits make out from the wood to the grass of the hillside. In the rough grasses of the hill are the roofed tunnels of voles that eat away the roots and leave the dried grass as a screen above their heads, so that they run secure from the keen eyes of owl and kestrel. Look again at the grass that grows long in the shade of the wood's fringe; the blades are nibbled, for the rabbits take those too. A thousand little incidents have left their story for you to read. Think, and use your imagination—not to make wild guesses but to imagine what a creature would be most likely to have done to cause what you find.

And now, I have not told you of foot tracks. They will certainly be there, if not at every visit, then at times. But foot tracks, I think, like food tracks, deserve a chapter to themselves.

May I tell you something else, not directly concerned with animals, though it has something to do with them?

Burrowing animals dig out at times more than mere earth and stones. Bracelets, brooches of gold worn hundreds, perhaps thousands of years ago, have been found lying at the entrance to a burrow. Coins, buried from sight for centuries, flint implements from the Stone Age, all have come to light.

What a treasure for you to find—rich in history even if it had little money value. Remember what I said— there are experts only too eager to tell you all about your find.

And now, I have chosen one example, a wood, of all the wonderful places there still are in our country for children to explore. Have I said enough to show you the way to set to work—enough to prove that a wood is not just a collection of trees to climb, or a good place for a den or a fire? But full of life—of voles, moles,

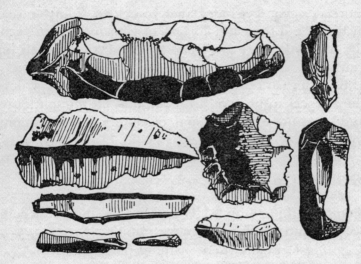

A few of the flints found in Epping Forest during the writing of this book. Scale about a half.

shrews, mice, fox, badger, stoat, weasel; visited and lived in by birds, beautiful with flowering plants and shrubs in their seasons, and splendid with the trees that make it what it is?

Don't expect to see everything at once. That would be impossible. Events take place in the world of plants and animals in appointed seasons. That adds to our pleasure, for nothing is ever quite the same twice running, and always something fresh is there for our seeing.

And now, before I leave this chapter, there are one or two things I feel I must say, concerning the friends that you will make.

You know how you respect the boy or girl who is kind to little brothers and sisters, and to pets. You respect them, you like them for it, you are glad to have them as friends for yourself. And you will find, and more so as you get older, that your love of any animal or bird, or of trees and flowers, or your interest in keeping fish, will make and keep friends for you wherever you go.

But there are things that people do to the very ones they expect to be good to them, and do thoughtlessly, and so cause suffering and often great loss. Among 'people' I include boys and girls.

Here are some of the things that hurt me inside to see done.

Standing Bottles on walls and tree-stumps and gate-posts, and smashing them with stones.

Lighting Fires anywhere, without permission.

Fouling Drinking Water in troughs and streams.

Cutting Sticks and barking trees and carving names in others.

Breaking Through Hedges, lifting out wire-fence posts and leaving them flat or loose.

Sitting on Gates so that they drop at the latch end.

Opening Gates and leaving them open.

Deliberately Letting animals from one field into another.

Walking Through standing crops; picnicking in them, playing in them.

Trampling Down seedling crops.

Removing Stones from walls and rolling them down-hill.

Trespassing to fish or to rob orchards.

Robbing Wild Flowers by armfuls.

Putting Cars and Cycles without a word on to some-body's land and, when asked to go, behaving as if you had bought the land.

Behaving as if you thought that every farmer should immediately stop work to attend to you.

Leaving Your Litter for him to clear up.

Making 'Funny' Noises at farm animals.

Chasing them, or Letting Your Dog chase them. (*Very* funny for the dog, but not for the cow whose milk yield is spoiled until her nerves are restored to normal, or whose calf is born before time, and dead. Nor funny for the terrified sheep whose lambs are born with difficulty, often deformed or dead.)

These are a few of the acts so many do without a thought for their effects. They well might make any countryman angry—indeed they do. And yet it is sur-prising how good-tempered he remains. Let me end with one true incident.

I was boating with my sister on the River Thames, when we saw a strange and inexplicable sight; a man coming along the bank towards us, bending down every few yards for just a second or so, then coming on again.

'Putting these into rat-holes,' he called to us. 'These' were bottles, and he had just pushed dozens of them into the riverbank. He didn't mind much, he said, but he could show us something he did mind.

So we tied up the boat and went with him. There we

saw his splendid river meadow, beaten into utter chaos. Hundreds of pounds changed almost overnight into scores of pounds. Trampled, played in, rolled in, camped in.

And he wasn't angry; only saddened that such ignorance could be. 'They didn't know,' he said, 'they came for a week-end's camping and a bit of fun. It was just a field of grass to them.'

And to how many people it would be 'just a field of grass'.

To you? I hope not.

Here is the farmer's most valuable crop, his standby for the lean months, a crop not to be taken again for a whole twelve months.

What right have we to be ignorant of such things, today?

One more word on country manners. Have you noticed boys and girls—yes, and some grown-ups too, talking as if they believe that farmers and country folk in general have to make conversation in a queer sort of English that doesn't exist anywhere in these islands? Very funny it is, they imagine, to talk as farmers do.

'Eh, Jarge, us'd be dungin' that there vield if on'y tud stop a pourin' zo.' 'Us varmers do speeak zo.'

Well they don't talk any such nonsense.

If you do come across people who speak a good broad dialect, then be proud and glad. Glad, for to listen is one of the joys of the country holiday. Proud, for out of these ancient ways of speech has grown the noble language that is ours today. You are listening to the speech of men long dead. While their speech lives on, strong and virile, ours is still a living language.

CHAPTER THREE

WARNINGS IN THE WILD

And One To You

Why, you may ask, should I bother to tell you about warnings. Since you don't carry guns, who or what is likely to bother about a boy or a girl?

Well, even though you carry no gun and nothing with which to do damage (and that is not true for all boys), many many creatures are going to note both you and your doings. They will see you and the manner of your coming, and they will pass on the story of your doings.

Is it not worth your while to know the story they are telling? To be like the Keeper who, standing hidden in a corner of his wood, can tell what is happening over all the wood, though he sees nothing but trees and the wild birds? You can learn to do the same with time and patience, and a mind that is willing to understand and be interested.

There must be a reason for these warnings, and the first and the one that colours our whole reception in the wild, is the fact that we are trespassers there.

'Oh,' but I hear you saying, 'I don't trespass.'

But we do, all of us, every time we go into the country.

There are no notices, no closed roads, no barbed

wire, no boundaries that we can see. But the boundaries are there, and over the area they bound, watch eyes, and listen ears, and twitch noses that must keep a constant surveillance.

A badger showed me how keen an animal's hearing may be. I saw her jump and heard her dash underground twenty feet away when I swallowed—and I scarcely heard myself.

A fox, as I moved my finger to take a 'flash' of him, heard my finger unstick from the torch-case it had been holding. Eight feet below, in the mouth of his earth, he turned to stare at me and we looked each other in the face. Then, without sound that I could hear, he vanished underground.

Wild creatures have probably keener scent than many domestic animals, yet a little mongrel dog I know can find me with ease an hour, or two hours, after I have left. In the open, with wind from you to it, a deer can smell you half a mile away at least.

In the wild, where animals are hunter and hunted, vigilance is the price that must be paid in order to remain alive. And when you remember that man has persecuted the wild creatures for centuries, can you wonder that warning is given of our approach?

Almost every square foot of land in these islands is lived upon or in, by some animal or other; many so small that they fall outside the scope of this book. But millions of Vertebrates live here too; yes, millions. And all have their territories, each animal with sufficient to support itself and to provide food and home for a mate and young family. Animals keep an unsteady balance of numbers, except where man interferes, or when, as does happen, something beyond the control of the animals themselves and not for their ultimate good makes their numbers increase out of all balance—that spells disaster. But generally speaking, the young born each year are enough to replace those that have died or been killed, with some to spare for the young and careless that are going to be meals for other animals.

For many of the babies born in the wild are going to die young, in their first few weeks of activity. If it were not so, the world would be for a short time over-run with animals; and then starvation and disease would do their work, as they always do in such cases, and wipe them out.

But because each animal has its own living space, it does not mean that it thereby has it selfishly all to itself. There may be many other creatures living there. Thus a deer will have other deer living on its food range because deer are largely herd animals. But there may be badgers as well, and squirrels and mice and hedgehogs, and many birds, all living there, but not as direct competitors for food.

And hunting animals will be found too, with territories overlapping the deer's and overlapping one another's. Fox and stoat, polecat and otter, each in its own way finding a living on the other inhabitants. But hunting, we should remember, is always a wasteful and extravagant way of living, and so hunters are always in a minority; one hunting animal to many hunted. That is something often lost sight of when Man makes up his mind to destroy a creature he feels is doing too much damage. And later on he himself has often to do the work the hunter would have done. It is always unwise to rush into methods of bettering Nature, whose schemes have slowly worked themselves into being as

Time grew old.

We have said that the surface of the earth is divided up; and the space above it, from the grasses to the very tops of the trees, is divided, loosely and with many over-lappings, among the creatures and the birds.

Think a moment, and you will see that it is so. How astonished you would be to see a mole endeavouring to climb a hedge; or to see the fierce little shrew, that kills worms and beetles, running up an oak trunk after a green long-horn grasshopper, that lives in oaks, though it may kill many a grasshopper on the ground.

There are certain habitats that we associate with definite animals, and rightly so though not rigidly so. And when you come to make a study of the birds of your countryside, no matter where you live, you will find they 'own' their layers of the air, not because they live there exclusively, but for the simple fact that there they obtain their living.

The earth, the trees, the air, all were divided up before man ever decided to make them his own pro-perty. He comes into a world teeming with life, with creatures and birds that depend for their very existence on knowing of danger in time; in time to make a sur-prise attack or to reach safety. And into this same world now come—you, representative of the race that has hunted mercilessly both bird and animal. And you, so huge, and clumsy and slow by comparison, are known at once as enemy.

You bend down. A rabbit feeding five yards out from the hedge sees you. He knows what you are doing; picking up stick or stone.

You point to the hedge. A blackbird sees you move hand and arm. He too understands; you are throwing something, to maim, to kill.

How can we make the wild creatures understand that we are doing nothing of the sort? It can be done by patience and by taking care that we never give reason to doubt our good intent. But until that time you will be seen and noted and warned about. Come quietly as you will (sudden quiet will give you away) you will be noticed long before you reach your watching place. Some living thing will have told of your coming when you were still in the far field by the corner gate.

Do I mean that the wood has been warned deliberately? That is perhaps saying too much. A ringdove claps out, and gives alarm. But before we say that it was deliberately warning other birds and animals, we must watch and think carefully. We do know of course that certain birds that fly together or that feed together, like geese on migration or rooks feeding in a field, give warning. But we have to be careful before we credit wild creatures with the thoughts and the feelings and desires of ourselves. But I am sure that the more time we spend with wild creatures, the more we shall come to think that they do communicate with one another. Think of the squirrels. They constantly utter little sounds that are lost a few feet away, at least to our ears, and yet other squirrels almost certainly hear them and understand their meaning. Keep a squirrel and you will soon learn to understand some of them too.

Go out alone, when you must depend on your own senses, and it will not take you long to learn alarm cries of bird and even of beast. Notes of fear and of pain are understood by every creature, no matter who utters them; and the cries of animals are understood no less by human beings.

A pied woodpecker cries sudden and sharp 'Chip, Chip, Chip, Chip!'—the yaffle sends through the wood a wild and ringing cry. Do we not understand these?

The vixen sitting watching with loving devotion her woolly-coated cubs, hears a step. She cries once, sudden and sharp; and we almost jump ourselves at the note of urgency. 'Whuuah!' she cries, and every cub has tumbled out of sight in a second. These are vocal warnings, voice warnings, that we all can comprehend.

But a warning has no need to be vocal. A badger tears back to earth at the snap of a twig. And at his thudding, every badger waiting in the mouth of his tunnel, nose to wind, learns of trouble above and acts accordingly. Animals and birds take the keenest interest in the actions of others.

I saw two great titmice feeding in an oak. One crouched, suddenly, to the branch; and as I watched, understanding but not seeing why, there floated through the sunlit trees the black shadow of a crow. As he passed near, the tit cried warning and his mate repeated it farther on.

But even without that call, any eye that had seen as I had seen, would have understood. Just as when a squirrel leaps from ground to tree and whisks around the trunk to hang immobile, every watcher knows there is danger.

A rabbit in a field lifts ears in sudden alarm. Do not you understand? And because a wood or a field does not burst into feverish activity at a signal, that is not to say the signal has passed unnoticed. Often the safest course in danger is to remain still, perfectly still.

I remember watching a rabbit. I was in a tree and the rabbit hopped out on to a mound below. Something, he decided, was in the tree but what he could not tell, so he settled down to wait, at least until whatever it was moved and so gave itself away. So I didn't move; I settled down to watch the rabbit instead, and to time him. And for forty minutes he sat unmoved, squatting on his mound, till other rabbits rushed out into the dusk and, racing past him, broke the spell; and we both felt able to move. Off he went, little white-tail in the dusk. Now supposing he'd done that before—run off instead of sitting still. Then he would have been plain to every foe nearby. Sitting down he had been almost invisible.

So warnings can work for both good and harm, and the wild creatures understand this; and many a bird that gives noisy warning otherwise, falls into soft and gentle voice at nesting time. And just as a cry of alarm betrays the maker, so a mark or movement may give away the owner.

You can read these signs, so why not spend an hour or two sometime, sitting quietly, reading all you can of them?

A handful of birds throws up along the fringe of a spinney. Up, like thrown grain it goes, but somehow it seems not to want to settle but to go on jerking higher and higher and wider and wider apart, till suddenly the whole flock slips down and out of sight in the trees. Then you may know the sparrow-hawk is sliding through on rounded wings. Do you not believe that every small bird that saw that scattering knew the reason why?

Or suppose it is just a human passer that comes. He goes by and never once suspects that you are sitting there. You may not even see him but you can follow his passage.

A blackbird slips out of the hedge and in again twenty yards farther down. A brown wren 'ticks' and threads a path through the maze of the hedge bottom. A robin forsakes his spray above the hedge and slips down to disappear into the grasses, tall in the shade. Farther down a whitethroat jerks up into the air and drops scolding in a steep dive behind the hedge.

And so it goes on all the way down. Not just where the walker is now, but ahead of him, until the gateway is reached.

There the ringdove slips out, not with a noisy clap of wings, for she has domestic affairs to think of, but swift and silently from the far side of the tree. A turtle-dove flies out from a maple in the next hedge and rises so that you can see the white band that edges his tail. He flutters up to settle on the telephone wire, hunched-back, and alert.

Don't move yet, for the hedge beyond the gate is suddenly full of commotion; of hurried leavings and re-enterings; of more birds than you dreamed were there. For the passer has stopped a moment in his walk, and made all the wild folk uneasy.

You have seen these things for yourself or others like them, and understood. They, with a thousand others, can become part of your 'field-knowledge', of your woodcraft, if you are willing just to be patient and observant, and if, whenever you see or hear something unusual, you refuse to be satisfied until you have at least tried to discover its cause. Be like the fox that never lets fear get the better of him but circles back after a fright to investigate and make sure for the future.

There will be other times when the warning is meant to be heard; and heard far and wide. These are the times when a squirrel—red or grey—is found too near a nest, or when a brown owl is found apparently asleep in his daytime roost. Then, the warning is a challenge to all around to come and join. Now, you may creep and watch for they have found a foe in need of urgent attention. See the squirrel flattened on his branch as if he grew there, but ready to dodge nimbly enough every time a bird makes a dive at him. See the old owl, sitting with closed lids, unmoved. See how the birds dive and brush near but never close enough to touch, till at last, unable to bear the hideous din any longer, he opens eyes, blinks slowly, drops from his perch, and floats to shelter more secure.

Have I, once again, said enough to make you want to go out, and commence your field-work—your real detective work? Then that brings me to the last warning in this chapter—the one to yourself.

You will be allowed, I am sure, to go off alone into the countryside without anybody at home bothering their heads with stupid and needless fears. I know I always was. But I had a time to be back and I know that I nearly always managed to miss it. Hours later, as I came into sight, there would be father or mother searching for sign of my safe return. For despite what I have said, parents do worry. I could see the shadow lifted from an anxious face as I arrived. That is something you can try always to avoid isn't it—needless anxiety caused to others?

And that brings me to the second part of the warning.

It is all very well for me to try to teach you how to

make yourself as invisible as possible, but there are times when somebody may want to find you—some one not so good at tracking, or less keen of hearing than yourself, or with eyes less trained.

You can help them, by letting them know where to find you if need be. Since you cannot do it so easily later on you must say where you are going, or leave a note to say where you have gone. It will rob your walks of no enjoyment; it may well mean that you will be allowed farther afield.

Not that anything is going to happen to you, of course it isn't. But all the same, accidents do happen. If anything does, it will be a comfort to you as well as to those at home if everybody knows that your word is to be trusted, and that where you said you would go, there you have gone.

Think it over.

CHAPTER FOUR

BIRDS

When Earl Grey of Fallodon wrote so delightfully of the birds he loved, he called his book *The Charm of Birds*. You may not read it till you are a little older but the charm of birds you know already, and you will discover it is a joy that grows with the passing of years and is enriched by observation and by knowledge.

Where must you go to study birds? To begin to learn them you have no need to go anywhere. Wherever you are they will be, even in the smoke of towns. If you are by the sea, then you have the shore birds that make music with their rippling cries as they run at the tide's margin. On the moors, the grouse hides in the heather and the dipper walks underwater in the hill streams. Or perhaps you are in the high hills with the mewing of buzzards and the splendour of the peregrine's flight. Or are you in town; then there will still be birds, if only the sparrows on the roof and the blackbird in the dusty laurels. They all have much to teach us.

Early men, by making wings of feathers, tried to copy the joy of flight which they beheld on every hand. Time and again, daring ones launched themselves into the air to crash to destruction. Boys and girls today can have no idea of how the wish to fly tortured for thousands of years the minds of men. Nor do they consider why the pioneers failed—and always must fail.

Could you explain it? Or have you ever wondered how a bird can come in from flight at forty miles an hour and stop in an instant and not be out of breath? How is a bird able to breathe at all in the high air in which it flies and to provide oxygen for all those muscles that must work the wings?

These are questions that call for study in books that deal with the anatomy of birds—the way they are built. There you will find the answer to why the goose and the crocodile have eggs so alike, and how it is that some nestlings have wing-claws that enable them to clamber about the nest and even to escape from it in time of danger. You will learn where the bones are that used to be the tail-joints—the vertebrae—in ancient birds.

It will help you to understand birds out-of-doors, if you have some knowledge of the path by which they have slowly become what they are, and of the problems which have been overcome to make them so.

Perhaps you will become an ornithologist—a bird enthusiast. More people take an interest in birds today than in all the other branches of the Animal Kingdom put together. Many are people who just delight to see and to hear them. Some are specialists, the only people who really add methodically to the world's knowledge. Some of them work in museums and with their skill in every little measured detail they make possible real identification and classification.

Some are photographers; others are patiently engaged in gathering records of migration and distribution. And some, I am afraid, think of little but their own gratification. They have forgotten that the bird has a life of its own and the right to live it. They have forgotten that if knowledge is not to add to the sum of happiness in the world, then it has no aim. In that happiness I am simple enough to include the birds'.

You are not likely to be measuring dead birds—indeed, if you find dead animals of any kind, you should always be careful to handle them with a stick, never with your fingers. But you are going to be out of doors, watching live ones, and there enthusiasm may be to the harm of the bird. Let me give you an example.

I met three young naturalists, all keen to become good ornithologists. They had joined the junior section of a very famous bird lovers' association in order to better themselves in their work. They were standing under an oak tree that held a sparrow-hawk nest. All around, the brambles were a trampled mass. One watcher stood in them while another climbed the tree, camera round his neck; the third waited on the path, binoculars dangling.

Now there was enthusiasm—but was there thoughtfulness? Was it a desire to help the bird that sent them there in broad day, in full view of passers? I can tell you what happened. Some other watcher came back later and took all five eggs—one of them pure white. There is always someone waiting for the chance to rob. That is a danger lurking for the bird or the mammal that becomes a friend. One year a Forest Keeper had a willow-warbler that would come to his hand to rest on the way to feed her babies. In the end somebody took advantage of the bird's confidence and robbed the nest.

For despite all I have said of the wariness of wild birds and animals, it is possible to make friends with them all. If you have them captive for some time, then it must be so, for otherwise they would not live.

What happens after, when they are gone back to the wild? People will tell you that wild birds kill those that have been caged; but I have known escaped budgerigars live for weeks in company with flocks of sparrows. They died at last, of hunger.

And I have had many birds that I have helped and then set free. Successfully? Yes, for some of them I know today, years after. And others I saw for a while after they were free and I watched them hunting for themselves.

My sparrow-hawk, seeing me come down the path to the trees he had adopted, would call excitedly. Then down he would dash to pick the meat from my enclosing fist with one hind claw. But when I went on holiday, he fed himself entirely and would never come to me again, though he would come down through the trees above my head. He had not forgotten, he had just learned to do without me. That was as it should be, for to me the bird is happiest in living the life for which it is fitted.

My brown owl, set free, has reared several families a few hundred yards away. She still found time, for several years, to come by night to hold converse with me in the ash tree beyond my window, waking me to call answer back, till her voice sank softer and softer to a whisper in the night air.

But how are you going to know all these birds in the field—to learn them?

Go, if you can, with someone who knows the birds and is willing to put up with all your wrong guesses and your questions. I went with my father, and he it was who opened my heart to the lore of the country. But there came the day when father left me to do my own watching. Then I learned the hard way. I had no book to give me field characters—those points to look for when you see the bird only at a distance. Bird-song records I had never heard of. I went out with a picture in my mind of all I could remember from bird books from the library. I soon found that what an artist had seen in a stuffed specimen I could not see out-of-doors. So when I saw a form unknown, or heard a new song, I spent patient hours creeping close enough to note the details. I had no binoculars, but I had been blessed with sight that could distinguish more than many could with glasses. And I trained my eyes, as I have trained the other senses we usually ignore. And if I learned the hard way, and the long way, at least I never forgot a bird I had once learned. Not only was its picture fast in my mind but my inner ear could hear again its song. And the whole scene, the day, the season, the tree, the distant view, all were part of my picture of the bird. So that now when I hear records of songs that to others pour forth from one soundbox, I see the living bird again as I saw it when I first learned it, and as I have heard it so often since. The wren trills his spring joy from the hawthorn thicket; the curlew's voice comes over the vast hills; the evening is golden where the blackbird sings. My world then, is far removed from radiograms and the comforts of indoors.

You, of course, have advantages I never had, and you must use them. But remember that the greatest joy will come from what you do for yourself. So many boys and girls I know, listen to wireless programmes and watch television shows—and are too tired to do anything for themselves. The man who mimics bird songs, took pleasure in learning them. The man who shows you wonders of plant or animal life, was himself thrilled to learn them. Unless you are going to follow up what you are told or shown with discovery of your own, you will never know the joy they knew.

Hear your records, know the song again, from sky or bush or tree, and then get to know the bird. Know every detail; its movements when singing or feeding, its posture at rest. Be able to tell it at a glance, by its flight, its movements in tree or on ground; the living bird. The lifting of a blackbird's tail, as it alights on a post. The jerking of a moorhen as it moves, the flicking of the white tail; the turns of the swift that are accomplished, as you can see for yourself, by the beat of one wing; the upright stance of that bold bird, the mistle-thrush.

When shall you start? In the autumn, if you can, or in the winter. Fields and gardens then are full of bird cries, even of song. The robin begins again in August, so does the songthrush; and whenever the days are mild enough, you may hear hedgesparrow and mistlethrush and wren and titmice all through the winter. And as the days steal round to smile at spring, and the lark sings over the brown burrows, others come into song—blackbird and chaffinch and greenfinch. These are the voices of our resident birds. With them you may learn the calls of migrants come to winter with us: the loose rattle of fieldfares about the ploughed lands, the cries of redwings moving restlessly by day and by night, the wonderful music of geese in a singing skein across the sky, heads towards the lands of snow. And every new song learned will be as a standard by which to compare and contrast; each will help to distinguish another.

There is nothing hard about learning bird songs: it only requires the will and the wish. Call to the birds as you go, and if you are a good mimic, they will answer.

The willow-warbler sighing 'Hueee' in the birch tops, will creep down through the branches to see who it is that calls. The greenfinch will wheeze and cry with tender melancholy; the thrush shout defiance from the trees; the robin come beside you, till you have left his domain, where he still sings with liquid, pure note.

And not only by day. The birds of the night will answer you too. Flight by flight through the dark trees, the brown owl will come, and call. Many and many a time I have brought them.

'PuhschWEEuh!' 'PuhschWEEuh!' I call, imitating the young.

'KeeooEEE!' 'KeeooEEE!' calls back the bird, staring with passionate intensity down. 'KeeooEEE'— 'KeeooEEE'—'KeeooEEE!' higher and higher, faster and faster, till at last the noise falters and breaks into a wheezy hoot, full of tenderness; and so ends.

The call of the young seems irresistible.

I had a young owl, taken, when it was just old enough to scramble alone, from Essex into Surrey. One day it escaped and hid all day. In the night it wakened us, calling 'PuhschWEEuh!' 'PuhschWEEuh!' to the dark wood below the house. And then from the wood, we heard the answer back: the call of a grown owl. Lying awake, we heard the two draw together, and the cries die and cease. And going through the wood the next night, we found the two, the old and her foster child sitting together in the dusk; and so they were left.

Let me tell you one little story to show you how easily

you may win the trust of a bird. One day I was brought a sparrow. To spare it from too much well-meant attention, I kept it in a cupboard till all was quiet at luncheon hour. Then I tried to feed it. It twisted, it turned, it pulled from my hand with frenzied strength. It was only a baby. I feared I should injure it so I put it back. Hours later it went home with me, nestled in a pocket.

There, I put it among the French beans, where many sparrows were doing my work for me, getting rid of blackfly from under the leaves. For hours I heard the young one's lusty cry among the beans. Next day he was there, and then he disappeared.

A week later, I was working on my allotment a quarter of a mile away. 'Look,' my wife cried, 'there's a young sparrow won't fly away.'

I went to look. There he was on a post, a young sparrow. I held out a finger. 'Come,' I called softly, 'come, little one.'

And he came. He came and sat on my finger while I chatted and all the sparrows nearby called to him from their freedom.

Was he my sparrow of a week before? How could I know?

If he was, then his was an amazing return for the little I had tried to do. If it was not he, then what he did was even more amazing; and it shows how simple and complete can be the trust of a bird that sees and hears that you are to be trusted.

It is time indeed that we were able to be taken on trust. Happily gone, we hope, are the days when whole races of gem-like birds could be exterminated to put on women's hats; days when to Englishmen it seemed fitting to do their bird-watching with a gun and a glass-case. We have no need today to bring our booty home to know it, for we can go easily and cheaply out to watch the bird—a living animal in its proper setting.

And if your bird-watching does nothing more than that, it will not have failed. Go into the English countryside with a heart that is thankful for so much of beauty left, a beauty in which the birds hold no small part.

CHAPTER FIVE

BIRD-NESTING

Bird-nesting, is it wicked—is it wrong?

How can I say either, when thousands of birds' eggs are taken every year for food (though many of them are the eggs of birds we should protect). How can I say it when farmers must go round the rookeries and thin numbers with a charge of shot for the sake of the crops (though the rook does the farmer great service through much of the year). When gamekeepers must in their daily work shoot birds and destroy their nests, in order to save game birds (though only to have them shot in the end).

You must decide for yourself whether what you are doing is good. But first let us look together at what bird-nesting can mean, what it has led to in the past; it may help you to make up your mind.

Imagine yourself, wandering down the hedges, taking an egg here, another there; all you took a fancy to, all you had not already. Squirrels and crows and jays are shot for doing that very thing; and yet they have some excuse, for they want the eggs as food.

What excuse have you? That you want them for a collection?

Well, up and down the country magnificent collections were made in the past—and afterwards no one wanted them. In any case, they were almost valueless.

Unless a field note-book was kept to give full details of each find, where today is the priceless knowledge that must have been possessed by the gatherers of those eggs? Gone beyond recall, and no one the wiser or the better for it.

If you do start collecting in real earnest, then you must go on till you have the egg of every common bird; and then—nothing will satisfy you but to have the triumph of holding in your hands what few besides can hope to have—eggs so rare, so precious to us in these islands, that your taking of them may mean the difference between a bird's continuance and its extermination. You will have come to the stage when no consideration will stop you; you will have become a collector. There are such people, whose hobby has degenerated into selfishness.

Collectors have had other forms of mania. One was the getting together of every egg of one species that showed variation. The blackbird was chosen, for her eggs vary in shape and size and colouring. But the collectors knew that before they began, and so did everyone who had looked into blackbird nests. Today, with the wonderful gift of colour photography, such a wicked waste will never, we hope, be undertaken again.

I would say of collecting in general, that it is, if nothing else, perfectly needless. There are plenty of collections of eggs for reference in this country and experts ready to help you with any problem. You need never worry, if ever you should come across a rarity, experts will be down to see it at once with their congratulations.

The only excuse I could understand for the taking of an egg, would be that you desired above everything to possess, if only for a while, so beautiful a thing.

But if everything beautiful is to be killed, even to go into a museum, how much poorer we all shall be.

When I was a boy, the understanding at home was quite definite; bird-nesting was forbidden, and that I am sure was the right decision. As we grew older the desire grew less. The more we learned of the lives of birds, the more we understood how Nature thins the numbers of young birds, as of all young lives, herself.

I saw this thinning during the summer. In a few yards of country road I came upon three dead sparrows, all in the first few months of life. On the far side of the road was a field of wheat in which they had been; a field that lay below the level of the road, without hedge or fence to bound it. The sparrows had flown straight from the wheat to their doom; each had been struck by a passing car. A fence, a hedge, and they would have had to rise: they would have been above the cars, and safe. And roads are only an artificial way of adding to the mortality Nature herself demands.

But surely there is something you can do, without adding to the death-roll, and yet share the joys of nesting time?

Of course there is.

Alter 'nest-robbing' to 'nest-watching', and your days will be full, and your note-book too; and so others may learn something of what you have found and cherished. Once you have watched a nest from its first making, through the laying, the hatching, feeding and the flying of the young, you will have no desire to rob any nest.

Nest-watching requires skill and patience; perhaps that is why the casual robber of nests seldom stops to learn; he has not the qualities that go to make a naturalist. When you go, remember that where you have been others will go, and all the more easily for your having shown the way; not by word of mouth, but by actions, and above all by the signs you leave behind you.

The trampled spray of bramble trodden down because it was in the way; the grasses at the bush edge, no longer standing straight as when you came; the withered and dried vegetation where you stood to watch; the torn bark and the broken twigs where you climbed for a closer view. If you wish to see the open 'gateway' you have left, come again an hour or so later, and see the difference made to all you damaged, by sun and wind. You will see it like a sign, 'Trespassers welcomed'.

To watch some nests you need of course leave no trace nearby. The nests of nuthatch or of woodpecker you can watch from afar, and better still if you have field glasses, so that you may see the food brought to the young and the young themselves at the mouth of the hole.

If the nest is in bush or thicket, then you may like to use a periscope, which will show you the interiors of nests far above your reach. But periscopes, we found, are apt to be noticed by everybody, so use them with care, and remember to keep out of sight yourself.

And since your motto is I hope, to be, 'Live and let live', remember to look around, not only when you leave your hiding place to see that everything is as when you came, but on arrival—to see how much tell-tale damage you left after all, on the last occasion. It may make you a little humble, and more careful.

Care, and patience, and endurance—the will to come

regularly and early—these are the qualities that bird-watching demands: and they are qualities worth acquiring. It takes far more to make a real study than to take an egg.

It would be so easy to do the wrong thing: no one is there to say, 'Don't!' No one need know.

This is the time when character shows: for what you do depends entirely on yourself.

CHAPTER SIX

IN WHICH I THINK OF ANIMALS

Whenever I am in town, although I see interest and beauty there and enjoy the friendly comfort of human homes, all the time I can see inside me the fields that stretch out from the last houses, and more fields beyond, with their woods and streams. Not empty fields and woods; not mere haystacks standing in the corner of the meadow; not just vast barns waiting hollowly for storing.

I peer in imagination into those barns, lofty and cool in the white light of the day. In the dusk within are rats that have burrowed a way in, to leave a little pile of fine earth against the foot of the wall inside, which tells of their coming. House-mice, with their musty smell, are here too. They sit up with fallen grains of wheat in tiny handlike paws and nibble unafraid; to whisk out of sight as the farm cat, eye pupils suddenly big and dark, steals in at the barn door.

Along the rafters, like tiny mummified black hams, hang bats upside down, waiting for the true dusk and the hours of moth and beetle. All day they hang in the twilight of the barn; and yet they know the hour when the sun draws to setting, by some subtle sense of the passage of time. A sense that once we possessed, and that we can cultivate quite easily, so that we may waken fresh and ready at any hour we will.

I stroll by the stacks of hay. There, mice have burrowed, and the grass-snake, following through their
tunnels, has made way to the thatch top, and lies there
in the hot sun, basking.

The grey rat, the despoiler, runs from the stack to
drink in the ditch bottom, and coming back finds a nest
of pipits in the grass, and devours them all.

Out in the fields are more rats, living free. One has
his store of winter potatoes in the ridge between the
furrows, a whole bucketful of potatoes filched from
the farmer's rows, to be a guard against the winter's
possibilities.

I see another, robbing the bushes round the soft fruit
plantation of a market gardener. The bushes are cob
nuts, and the rat has a store of pounds of nuts, hidden
in the compost heap in the corner by a wall.

The fields and their hedges are full of animals and
their homes. The mole has his tumps there; the voles
are there, with teeth that never root, but grow through
life that the little gnawer may feed on the coarsest of
grass food. Wherever their food grows, and there is a
piece of discarded wood or a length of rusty corrugated
iron lying on the ground, there you will find the voles
congregated beneath.

There are rabbits, too, that steal from the hedge to
hide in the corn; and after them comes the weasel, with
sinuous curve and loop of body, and his little bright
triangular head lifted inquiringly.

So, as I walk in the towns, I know the fields, and my
heart is there. I shall not be really quiet of mind, till I
have been to them again. There I can walk and call to
the birds that sit in hedge or tree. I may sit, without
any wondering why, till the trembling field-mouse

comes to my shoe, and climbs unafraid as to some new-found stone.

I will walk slowly by the field hedge, where in the bank the rabbits have their warrens; a maze of tunnels that will at last cause the hedge bushes to collapse into the ditch below, or the fence to sag and sway drunkenly.

There is a spinney at the corner of two fields, and there a fox has been asleep in the filtered sun of afternoon, where he lay in the lee of a thicket. But he has heard my coming, and six feet deep in his earth, brush tip over nose, ears sharp, he watches for my shadow to pass over the mouth of the den.

A stream with banks deep-cut by its winter floods, runs through the spinney. Following its winding course leads a pathway, some four inches wide and trodden smooth by many nights of comings. For this is the badger's nightly path. Down the edge of the corn in the far field goes the path, down to the bank at the bot-

Badgers making love-play in autumn. From a flash photo. (Epping Forest)

61

tom, where a few gaunt thorns stand as windbreak, and the only fence now is of barbed wire.

There in the bank is a gaping hole, where two nights ago the badger came and dug out a wasp nest, and made havoc of the whole ingenious construction, and crunched up the enraged wasps and all their fat white grubs. Today, only a few lonely insects fly disconsolate in and out. Their tragedy, that seems so complete, is not yet played out.

In wasp and in bee nests, below their living quarters dwell a humbler race that feed on the fallen waste and the droppings from above. These are the Volucella larvae, grey and spiky grubs of flies.

They are in the débris now, as the wasps come in to alight and crawl towards the rear of the nest, where still a few cells remain. The grubs are starving; here is meat. They rise from the grey powdered scales of the ruined nest and seize upon the hapless wasp. This is an embrace from which there is no escape. The wasp may whirr with frantic wings, and bend its poison-pointed abdomen round to try to reach. The grubs wrap their bodies round the thorax, and all the strugglings of the wasp avail it nothing, it is dead already.

For the scavengers, the menial devourers of frass, have turned on their overlords, and become master in their house.

Not far from the wasp nest, in the rough turf at the edge of the path, lie little tough brown objects like pots, strewn in a litter of dry grass. This, until a few nights ago, was the nest of a humble bee that Brock scooped out with one sweep of his front paw; and here he feasted well on bees and bee-grubs, and on the honey that was to be the precious food for the colony.

But a hedgebank has more than bees and wasps. It is a highway for many small mammals. Here the stoat skips out and, seeing an intruder in his hunting grounds, sits up to watch; white shirt front, hands down-hanging by his chest like a tiny kangaroo. Seeing me stand still he whisks off among the trees, black tail tip bushed out in annoyance and half-fear; for so he has seen the Keeper stand.

In the grasses of the bank is a little gathering of snail shells, all empty. No thrush has eaten these—was it hedgehog or vole? I pick one up and, at a glance see it is vole. The hedgehog crunches manfully through to the titbit that had felt itself so secure in its citadel of lime; but the vole drills neatly down one spiral of the shell. This was a bank-vole, and the snail the common garden-snail. But the field-vole eats snails too, the brightly-coloured land-snails.

Beyond the bank in a clearing are shrews, squeaking shrilly. I stand with feet close to them, one on each side of a shrew I cannot see but only hear. And without my seeing, it passes under my shoe and is twelve inches away before I suspect that it has moved.

Tragically brief, it once seemed to me, is the span of a shrew; perhaps a year of life. But into that time, what a life it has crowded. A frenzied round of killing and gorging, of sleeping, and waking to kill and gorge again and, somewhere, find time for family affairs.

We often waste pity on tiny creatures. But creatures that live long often do little more than exist. Smaller ones burn out their tiny bodies with incredible activity. So with the shrew.

I peer again into the grasses, thinking perhaps to see one tugging with beetle, or worm longer than itself. But

I see nothing, only hear those tiny piercing squeaks that tell me I am not so quick as they.

Out in the fields beyond, there are hares, russet tinged, with ears blacktipped.

Beyond the fields, again, there are deer in the woods, deer so wild they are not seen once in a month, except by those who have learnt their ways. To know of their presence I must look for slot, the hoofmarks of deer. Then perhaps I will come again, as I have come so often, and live again the thrill of the fight, when in the autumn the deer call and fight. These are fallow deer, escaped from a park, and they fight not to kill but to triumph.

In May, they lost their antlers, and till now they have been growing strong and lusty for this hour; fit and splendid after the summer feasts. They lower heads; the neck that is so thick seems twice its size and strength, magnified again by the mass of hanging hair. They charge, head almost to the ground. They dodge, they feint. They crash together, with forward-pointing tines interlocked. They heave and strain and grunt and shove. The ground heaves and thuds and trembles by them. Their breath hangs over like a shifting cloud of vapour. They swing their heads; they strive to throw their opponent. Bent are the great hind legs; the whole body from head to haunch curves like a bow. They strive till it seems no muscles can withstand that on-slaught.

Suddenly one gives way; he stumbles and is down— only to leap up and fight with double strength. But the other is master and presses his advantage home. Quite unexpectedly the end is here, and the buck that is beaten retires discomfited.

And there in the September days, so blue and gold, the does lift inquiring heads from their browsing and gaze at their new master. Master, unless some other buck can take his wives away, for this is but the beginning of the rutting season, for which the antlers were new-grown.

In the wood, are one or two old antlers still lying in the leaves, gnawn almost out of recognition by the does and by squirrels, rats, rabbits and mice.

The wood is full of life and its signs, if I can only find the time to come again. There are squirrels in the trees and hedgehogs in the thicket snoring till the dusk and the hour when they may waken to pick the slug from the edge of the fungus it is rasping away; the hour of beetle and of worm; the hour when the bat moth-hunts in the trees above.

In the streams are otters. Under a tree, a willow with a hollow trunk, I have found their footprints in a maze about the water edge. But the fish floating downstream on its side is not an otter kill. For on each flat side is a long scar, where the javelin beak of a heron held it in the muddy shallows but let it slip at the coming of the farmer's dog, hunting for water-voles in the rushes of the bank.

Now the fish can only die, for there is a film of white fungus where the beak cut through scale and skin. And there, on the stream bank, are many castings of heron meals; bones of fish and frog, bleaching in the sun, and glinting among them the broken pieces of water beetles snapped by the heron as he stood.

All these things I have mentioned, I have seen within a few miles of the greatest city in the world, London.

There are other creatures I have not spoken of yet:

Spoor of a St. Bernard dog; nearly registered. Natural size.

the toad that lays its rope of twin eggs in the ponds in March, but which may live far from water in the heats of summer. Then you may find it many feet up in a tree, or hidden in the beech leaves where, in the soft leaf-soil, it has hollowed a space for its body.

There is the frog, which seeks out the shallower parts of the pond, and there lays great masses of spawn outspread like the top of a table.

Through the grasses of the meadow slides the ringed snake, to swim with lifted head to the island in the pond. In the marshes it may find newts and frogs, and fish in the pond. Yet grass-snakes can live far from water, and you may hear their dry rustle in the bracken, and over leaves, and in the parched grasses of high pastures.

There are lizards that love the warmth. The slow-worm basks on the sandy path, the common viviparous lizard runs in the heather stems. So dry they are, the brittle lightness of the lizard's step sounds loud.

But for all their love of the sun and the desert days lizards, like snakes, are thirsty creatures, and you may find them running in the coarse grasses of the swamp or over the sphagnum moss of the bog itself.

When the hot days come in June, and the ponds dry up, they find there the cool dampness that they need. On the pond floor of black oak leaves, lie boughs from the trees above; branches that long since fell into the water and becoming heavy with its weight, sank.

There, beneath the logs, are the lizards; scores upon scores of them—females with black-pointed tails to show they have met danger and escaped with only the loss of the true tail. They wait in the dim wet for their families to be born. Pick one up, and it clings with bulldog bite to your finger, but harmlessly. It shows the dauntless spirit of the little lizard that will run out into the blinding eye of the sun over the snow or bask in the August suns.

As summer advances the grass-snake hides its eggs in the vegetation left in the corner of the field after the cleaning of the ditch; and having laid them, leaves them.

The adder brings forth her young; and the baby adder, seven inches long, betrays the nature of the reptile that, with no anger against mankind or any animal, yet has no fear of either because of the power of its strike.

Pick one up, beautiful in brown, and lozenged in darker brown, and it will strike in the flash of an eye, though no venom is yet stored above the hollow tooth. In the hot days the snakes are born and must drink.

When the dew is on the grass tiny adders drink. It is often the only water they can find.

The shepherd kills the vipers for the damage they may do to his flocks. But the countryman turns his hand against every thing that looks like snake. The harmless yellow-collared grass-snake is battered to death. The little slow-worm, the benefactor of mankind, is smashed underheel, or chopped in two with the handy spade.

The slow-worm, most inoffensive of creatures, moves gently through life; this is perhaps why they live so long, for when the farmhand was a boy the slow-worm was already in the field.

We kill so many creatures, and we kill them needlessly, both out-of-doors and in. In the fields the act is done in ignorance, it is swift, it is sure. But what of the

Viper or adder and two grass-snakes. To keep snakes and lizards perfectly still, hold the hands over them until they cease moving, then remove the hands.

thousands of young creatures brought home to die? They make no complaint. They fade away before our eyes; slip out of the world and the life they were born to enjoy. I still believe an animal is happiest living the life for which it is fitted in perfection.

See the vixen gazing at her cubs with a proud love that is very close to human joy. See the little chiffchaff, first wanderer from Africa to welcome the spring. He sits on his dead bough, punching out his little song with throbbing throat. At every note he turns, to see that no danger lurks that might harm the precious nest below.

Do you think they would willingly exchange their life for yours? Let us not imagine that because our life is happy it is the way of life that other animals would choose.

Let us go to the fields and the woods with hearts ready for friendship, and learn there how creatures really live. And when you grow up, let it not be ignorance and prejudice that decide for you whether an animal shall exist with you.

Your knowledge and your tolerance of mind must be their friend. You will, I hope, join those who believe that the power to kill gives us, not the right to do so, but a great responsibility to think carefully and justly before we reach for trap or gun, or snare.

CHAPTER SEVEN

FOOD TRACKING

Bird and Mammal

This chapter can be only a word or two of all that might be written of the food habits of wild birds and animals.

I hope it will make you go out, and look for yourself. So little is known. And the birds and the animals I have spoken of, the very trees that feed them, may not grow near you. But your animals feed on what the land provides, just as they make their homes of the materials they find to hand.

Let us not go in the rich days of summer or of autumn. Let us go together on a winter's day; an inch of snow hard on the ground, and a wind whipping off it to pick chill through the warmest clothes. A day to be glad out-of-doors. For we can know that after exercise with its sharp edge to appetite, there will be food at home and the welcome of warmth.

But what of the birds and the animals? The birds must feed and drink—or die, as so many die whenever frost locks land and water. Of the animals, some are sleeping, though even the soundest sleeper may waken to wander through a desolate world where no food exists. The hedgehog crunches crustily over the frozen snow. The lizard under the hedge runs on frozen leaves.

But they are not feeding. The lizard finds again an earth cranny unfilled by snow or burrows down into

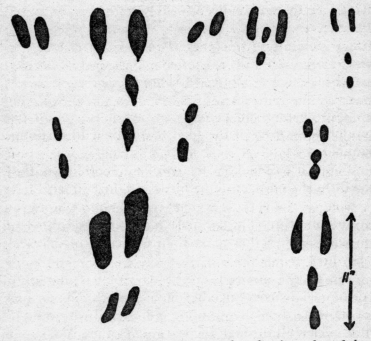

Rabbit tracks in snow taken on the same day, showing a few of the variations it is possible to find in a small area.

the leaves. The hedgehog finds a hole snug enough to keep frost from plucking his spark of warmth away, and falls again into death-like slumber, into a sleep so cold the snow lies on his coat unmelted.

But there are creatures out and feeding, for their tracks are everywhere in the snow. The rabbit has crept from his warm burrow to nibble the bark of the birch saplings. In the open, between saplings and burrow, his tracks betray his fear, for they stretch out longer and longer, the farther he went, till they make almost one long line of prints.

The squirrel has been out too; grey squirrel and red frisk over the crisp snow as if they were born and bred in it. Even in snow they may find food. There are fungi growing on the trees. The remains of tree harvests hang there still, clear etched against the blue sky.

When these have fallen, they have other, secret hoards. The red squirrel has his hidden in a tree hole, and both have hidden acorns and beech-mast scattered in the ground. Do they find these? Why should they bother? So long as they find with their noses a nut underground, why should they bother whether they hid it, or the falling leaves?

Now, in the snow, are little dark circular pits where squirrels have dug down with forepaws and unearthed the store.

In little hands the squirrel holds his food and, with minute thumb, deftly turns it for husking. If the acorn is ripe, the husk falls away in halves; if not, it is torn off in shreds from top to bottom. But that is not enough. The squirrel must take off the testa, the inner skin that covers the acorn itself.

These pieces you may find easily enough, for the eater takes no care to hide them; where he fed, they are left. He likes to feed off the ground. An old mole tump, an ant-hill, will serve. But best of all he likes a log, or the stump of a tree. There he will come day after day till the log is littered with the remains of his meal; for he is a wasteful feeder and drops many pieces, not only of acorn, but of beech-nut and sweet-chestnut, of hazel,

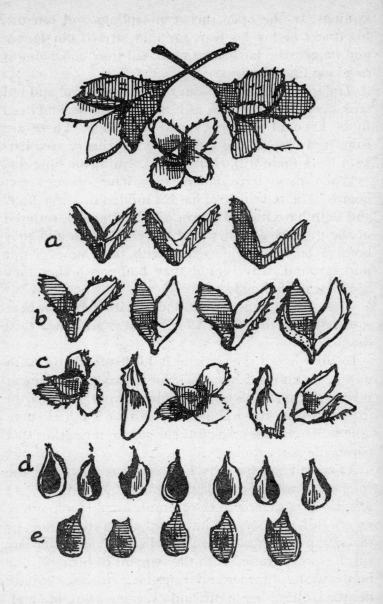

a

b

c

d

e

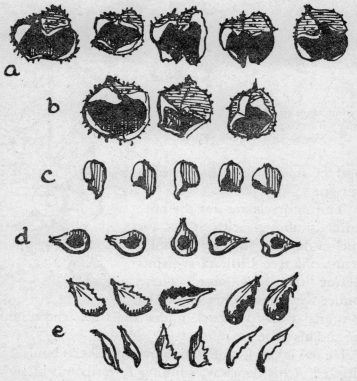

Above: Beech nuts, *a* and *b*, 'mast' collected when young, top nibbled away by long-tailed field-mouse; from a hole in an oak tree, 6 feet up, and from under logs. *c*, Nuts from same husks; *d*, Beech nuts pecked by titmouse; *e*, Beech nut fragments from store of long-tailed field-mouse. Natural size. (Epping Forest)

On left: Beech nuts. The red and grey squirrels' method. *a*, *b* and *c*, Husks sliced by incisors of squirrels; *d*, Nut with one side sliced off; *e*, Removed side. Natural size. (Epping Forest)

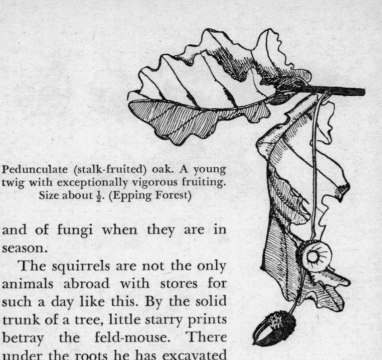

Pedunculate (stalk-fruited) oak. A young twig with exceptionally vigorous fruiting. Size about ½. (Epping Forest)

and of fungi when they are in season.

The squirrels are not the only animals abroad with stores for such a day like this. By the solid trunk of a tree, little starry prints betray the feld-mouse. There under the roots he has excavated a tunnel that runs back under the tree, where both he and his store are safe.

He too is careless of who knows his whereabouts, for littered at his doorway, running inwards out of sight and overflowing on to the open ground beyond his door, are the nibbled remains of fruits; the stones of the tiny wild cherry; the seeds from haw and from holly, mingled with the nibblings of acorn and of beech-nuts; and, in their hundreds, the little nuts of the hornbeam.

How good the hornbeam kernel must be, for every bird and creature near seems to enjoy its delicacy. And yet it is tiny, and the shell hard indeed. So hard that the seeds lie for two years on the ground before the rains

76

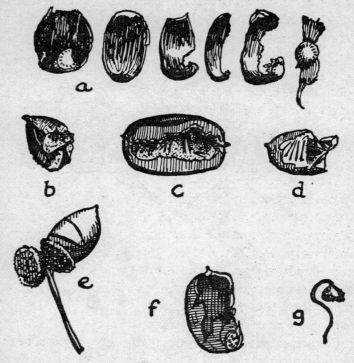

Acorns of pedunculate oak, from Epping Forest. *a*, Husk as left by squirrel; *b*, Acorn gnawed by squirrel; *c*, Acorn eaten by rabbit; *d*, Acorn attacked by titmouse; *e* and *f*, Jay's method, pecked at on branch; *g*, Discarded radicle always left by beast and bird. The radicle is little more than a water-tube and flavourless. Natural size.

Young acorns with tops drilled away; from feeding-place of long-tailed field-mouse below pollard oak. Natural size. (Epping Forest)

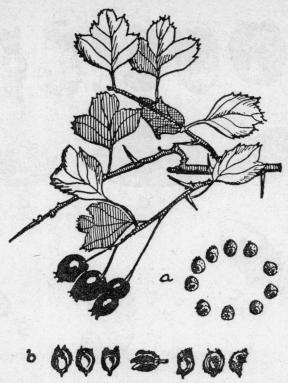

Hawthorn. *a,* Nibbled seeds from store of long-tailed field-mouse; *b,* Eaten by squirrel. Size ¾. (Epping Forest)

have softened them for germination. Finch and squirrel, mouse and nuthatch, take all they want, and yet there remain plenty to start into growth. The tree itself, in a good season, is prodigal. Two hundred and forty nutlets in one foot of branch. One thousand six hundred and eighty in one small squirrel-bitten spray. No wonder the field-mouse gathers them from the leafy floor, to enjoy them in the winter days.

But not all mouse stores are thus easily obtained. Six feet up in an oak another has his home, not for the sake

Holly. Seeds from old bird's-nest nibbled by long-tailed field-mouse. About $\frac{3}{4}$ size. (Epping Forest)

of the acorns, for the tree is past bearing, but for the beech-mast he has stored in the hollow bole.

Yards away the beeches stand, and every nut meant that he must climb the great trunks, the massive limbs, and out to the twigs to bite off the unripe fruit. Yet year after year mice have used that hole, till the beech husks, close nibbled round their tops just sufficiently to allow the incisors to reach within, spill over and litter the leaves below.

By a log are more mouse prints, blurred in the softer snow blown against the trunk. Turn the trunk and

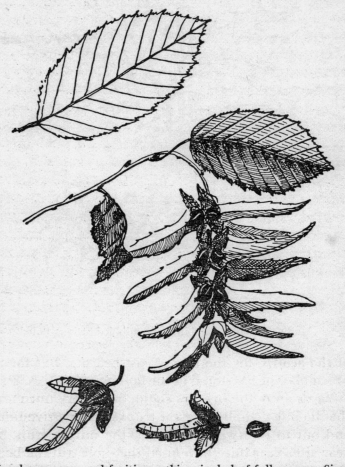

Hornbeam spray and fruiting catkin; single leaf fully grown. Size $\frac{3}{4}$.
(Epping Forest)

Above: Holly bark damaged by fallow deer. *Epping Forest.*
Below: 'Noccy,' my pet bat.
Photos J. W. Mellish

FOOD HABITS
Above: Feeding stump of grey squirrel (note food remains and scratchings from claws).
Below left: Toadstool attacked by slugs.
Below right: Toadstool attacked by grey squirrel. *Epping Forest.*
Photo J. W. Mellish

OD HABITS

ve: A quarter of the rat's store of cobnuts (found by D. Pettegree, Esq.).
to *J. W. Mellish*

dle: Snail shells nibbled by voles.
to *J. W. Mellish*

ow: Common lizard devouring house-spider (note shreds of lizard slough). *Epping Forest.*
to *E. Granger*

FOOD HABITS

Above left: Fox droppings (note 'beetle-droppings' of cubs).
Above right: Dung Beetles. *Epping Forest.*
Photo J. W. Mellish
Below: Remains of fox-feasts (note celluloid ring on leg). *Epping Forest.*
Photo J. W. Mellish

~OMES
~ove: Badger bedding bundles (Dec./Jan. '51). *Epping Forest.*
~oto *J. W. Mellish*
~ddle: Three badger cubs below 'watching-tree.'
~low: Two frightened cubs (one gone below). *Epping Forest.*
~tos *E. Granger*

HOMES
Above: The fox. *Epping Forest.*
Photo J. W. Mellish
Below: 'Watching-tree' above badger earth.

SOME OF MY EPPING FOREST FRIENDS
Above: Three grass-snakes 'waiting for instructions.'
Below: Grass-snake and slow-worm.
Photos S. E. Hutchinson

Above: Skulls from earths. *Epping Forest and Surrey.*
Photo J. W. Mellish
Below: Two friends that returned to the wild.
Left: My young sparrow-hawk.
Right: A young cuckoo.
Photos by Dr. W. Anthony

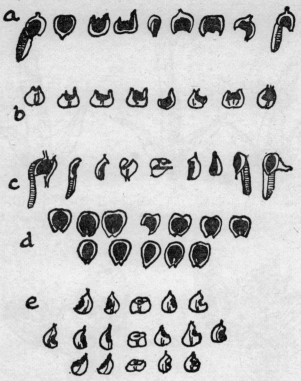

Hornbeam fruits. *a*, Nutlets attacked by red and grey squirrels in summer; *b*, From oak bark where wedged and broken by nuthatch; *c*, As eaten by greenfinch in summer; *d*, As eaten in winter, split by hawfinch, greenfinch and chaffinch; *e*, Nibbled by bank-vole and long-tailed field-mouse. Natural size. (Epping Forest)

Cherry stones dropped on a garden lawn and attacked by field-mouse. Natural size.

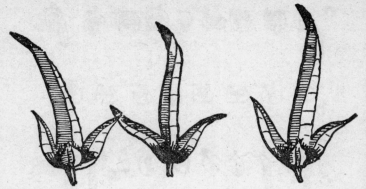

Hornbeam fruits stripped and dropped by grey squirrel, from catkin. Natural size. Note variations in length of wing; cf. p. 75.

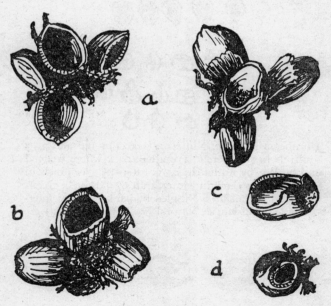

Hazel nuts from Bassenthwaite in the Lake District. Natural size. *a, b* and *c,* Attacked by red squirrel; *d,* Attacked by long-tailed field-mouse.

you would find his secret. For underneath are long passage-ways made by the groove and furrow of the hornbeam trunk. There the mouse has both home and granary; a round ball of shredded leaves and thin grass for home, beech and acorn for store.

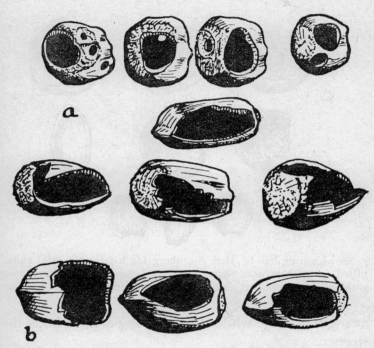

a, Cob nuts nibbled by Mr. Leutscher's hibernating dormice at South Kensington Natural History Museum; *b*, Cob nuts attacked by grey rats. Natural size.

Leave the Essex country I know so well. Come to the Lakes. There in the woods are hazel, and there the red squirrels have been feasting mightily. The squandered remains are everywhere; nuts torn asunder for the rich kernel, yet many wasted, untouched. For the red squirrel knows how to feast, to waste and be merry, as his grey cousin feasts and squanders, in southern copse and hedge.

In the litter of brown husks, are others, neatly filed away into a smooth hole. Here the dormouse climbed

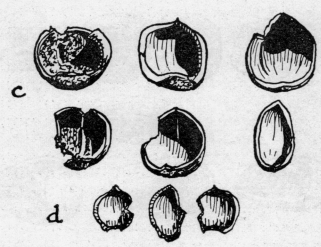

c, Spanish nuts left by Herr Swanberg for his famous wild thick-billed nutcrackers near Skara, Sweden; *d*, Swedish wild hazel nuts gathered by nutcrackers and buried in sphagnum moss. Natural size.

at night and ate while the other slept. Now he is the sleeper.

Where the lane climbs, are the pines; and here too the squirrel has been. Squirrels both red and grey enjoy the rich and oily seeds from pine cones. They strip the scales to find them, holding the small end where no seeds are, and so leaving a tuft by which to know their work. What if winter covers all trace of his autumn work, the squirrel can find more cones—enough for all the days of the longest winter.

Spruce cone from Germany.
Natural size.

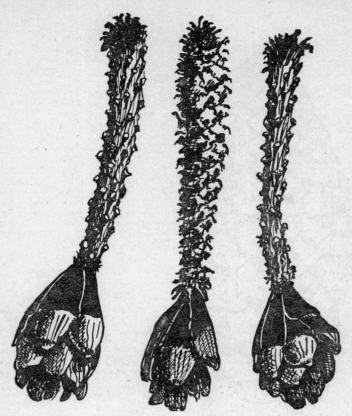

Spruce cones from Germany and Sweden, stripped by red squirrels
for the sake of oily seeds. Natural size.

But is there no animal abroad but squirrel and
mouse?

Here in the thin snow are tracks, the prints of a sow
badger. She has been out searching for food, for it is
January, and the tiny young that will be born in
March are growing within her. What food can she find,
this grey beast like a bear? Here we may see; for she has
been digging through the snow into the gravel slope:

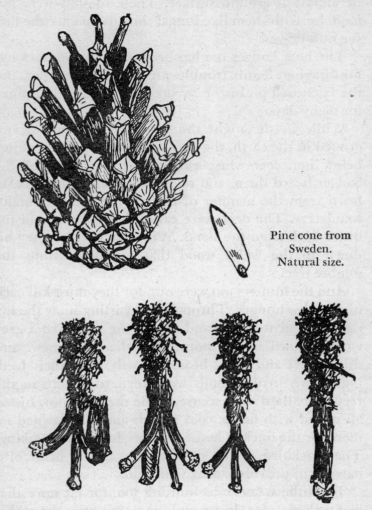

Pine cone from
Sweden.
Natural size.

Pine cones, stripped by red and grey squirrels for oily seeds. *Red*,
Sweden and Germany and Lake District; *Grey*, Surrey. Natural size.

into the fine soil where the slender rootlets of the beech lie almost at ground surface. These rootlets were her food, for with them live fungal threads that are the diet she now craves.

The boar badger too has been out. But he cares less for foraging; family troubles are no trouble to him, and the fat stored on his heavy body could keep him alive for many days.

While in the night the sow badger grunted, and groped in the earth, the deer were passing in the valley below her, feet whisper-light in the snow. But the badger heard them, and raised her head in inquiry, to learn from the manner of their going of other night-wanderers. The deer were eating holly leaves and the bitter bark from the stems. With strong teeth they bit down to the white wood that gleamed within the sombre tree.

And the hunters too were out, for they must kill each night or go hungry. Through the swirling snow the fox ran out, tail to wind, and passed the deer like a grey wraith blown in the storm. But the deer knew, and shifted feet and lifted heads uneasily from their feeding. Down to the ponds went reynard, where in the reeds a mallard slept secure, while the new snow hissed all round with fierce, cold sound; and day dawned no more for the duck. There was other food for his taking. The blackbird puffed out in sleep in the heart of a hawthorn; the vole, drunk with cold.

The lithe weasel was hunting too, for fat mice that had turned in for sleep: and the stoat was in the rabbit bury.

The hunters would soon forget their caution, and come into the yards where man had locked chicken and duck and goose. And the farmer, seeing the prints in the morning snow, would place a gun handy, knowing that the creatures to live must hunt, but not his stock, while he had a word to say.

And what of the birds? The birds that lay up no vast stores of winter fat but are opportunity feeders, feasting in times of plenty, starving in the hungry days, even in the very places where they wasted the harvest of the year? The birds must drink and feed, or perish.

Let me tell you of one winter, the winter of 1946–7, when blizzards held the land for weeks, and there was no fun for boys and girls in snow, for it lay and lay till it seemed it would never melt and go.

That winter, the larks came to us; to the fields just beyond the reach of London's houses. I saw them in hundreds of thousands; larks from beyond the North Sea. They came in search of fields as yet uncovered by the snow. There was none; but there had been cornfields raggedly gathered, with weeds standing even now with dry and rusty heads that whistled in the gales.

Thither came the larks to feed on the seeds of docks and plantains, and to sleep in the snow in the shelter of their stems. And over them the blizzards howled by night and day.

The water-vole, creeping up to the nearest tree to scrape down to grasses that were strangely green below, heard the larks purring in soft chorus overhead.

And a strange bird came to the marshes with his mate, and together they floated and soared in beautiful buoyancy of flight, for they were short-eared owls that had not been seen on the marsh for many years, not perhaps since that piece of London was built. Over the feeding larks they glided, over the vole half hidden by the snow-puffed branches of the tree. And the vole escaped and the larks. For were there not rats—many rats and gaunt—that killed and ate the larks as they lay dying in the snow? And the owls ate the rats, and they ate the voles that lived most of the winter days in a stupor under the snow. Two barn owls came and took possession of a ruined shed, and lived there all winter,

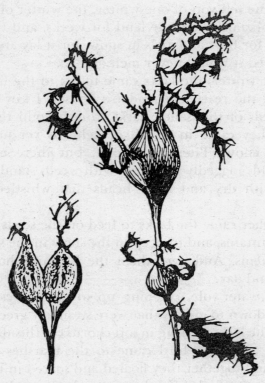

Thistle gall; drawn on Christmas Day. *Left,* Opened to show pupae which form a food supply for winter birds. Size about $\frac{2}{3}$. (Epping Forest)

to glide out in silent beauty and feast on more rats and the mice of the shed surrounds. Day by day I collected their cast pellets and opened them to find the remains of their hunting.

And fieldfares came, and flew with white axillary feathers flashing in the sun when winter shone like a jewel in the snow. They fed on haws till the bushes were stripped; and then they passed on farther south and west, or died in their sleep.

And the little Scandinavian redwings died, that had come with the opening of October and had shared the haws with the fieldfares. When the berries were all gone they sat in the bushes till night blew out the frail lamp of their life. They died, beside starlings that had sat for weeks puffed on their perches, dead and frozen to the twigs. And thrushes died, and blackbirds.

And yet, many birds lived. Finches and the linnets, that sought the seeds of weeds, they survived; and when the snow glistened and shone in a February sun, the linnets sang a sweet chorus to the spring that seemed past hoping for.

The little tree-creeper that seems without weight found food sufficient to support his body strength; spiders and spider cocoons, and woodlice where the bark was rotten and half detached, and torpid flies, so bloodless and dry they did not freeze in the bitterest day or night.

Titmice hunted in the trees, and dug into bark and buds and found eggs and sleeping insect life to feed upon. Woodpeckers jabbed with strong bills into bark and galls for larvae of beetle and wasp-fly. The nuthatch found odd seeds and fruits and jammed them in the jagged ends of split branches and into bark cracks, and split them open.

Hawk and owl found food where birds flew too weak to escape, in rat and mouse and vole. And as the hawks hunted, so the stoat and weasel hunted, finding frozen sustenance, bags of bones held together by drawn skin, yet sufficient to keep death away.

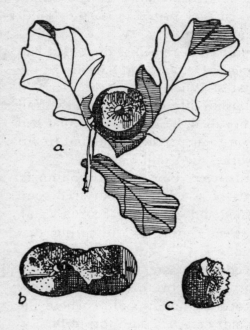

Marble gall on pedunculate oak. *a* and *b*, Attacked by birds for sake of grub within; *c*, Attacked by red and grey squirrels (teeth marks on surface). Size $\frac{2}{3}$. (Epping Forest)

And so that winter passed as every winter passes. The spring leaf burst upon the tree, the flowers opened on the bank below. The ice went from pond and stream; insect and flower were born together.

The squirrel and the finch bit off the opening leaf and the tasselled catkin on the tree; but it made no difference. The trees were green, the earth grew bright with grass; the birds found heart to sing.

And now, if I can tell you of the winter days that are times of scarcity, surely you can find how the birds and the creatures fare in the rich days, when all the world should be out-of-doors?

CHAPTER EIGHT

FOOT TRACKING

Bird and Mammal

Slowly but surely and ever faster now, we draw close to the birds and the animals we shall find at the end of the trail.

We have found their footprints, sure sign of their recent presence. We must learn to recognise them and know something of how to read them.

But you will not find here a description of all that you may find; that is the work that you will do for yourself. I want you to use your eyes, and to think for yourself. The more you use your eyes, the keener and the more alert they will become.

Footprints are everywhere, but few are the eyes that read them, beyond the trained glance of poacher and Keeper. The day when we needed to know them, the time when on our prowess in the chase depended the comforts of life and life itself, all this is gone. Well-fed content has made us forget to look, as our ancestors needed to look.

The fox prowls with light step in the farmer's yard and crosses to sniff the hen-roosts and try the catches there. And in the morning, coming in to work, the farm hands mistake the small prints for those of the terrier from the house or of the farm cat as she took

a, Print of dog-fox in earth **entrance**.
b, *c*, More usual prints.
d, Cat print. All natural size. (**Epping Forest**)

Above, Forefoot of dog
of greyhound type.
Below, Hind foot; feet
spread in mud.
Natural size.

Tracks of sow badger. Natural size. *Above*, Left hind foot registered, i.e. covering forefoot. *Below*, Forefoot.

Tracks of forefoot of boar badger on two different days on the same path. Natural size. From casts made by J. Gomer, Esq., in Epping Forest.

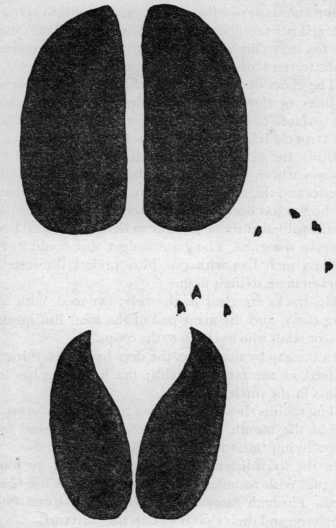

Cow tracks, half-size, with track of rabbit, natural size, showing four claws on right forefoot and three on hind foot.

herself off for a night's rabbiting.

But the claws of a fox are not the short blunt claws of a dog. They are fine and curved and sharp. With them the fox may climb a tree and gaze down unperturbed at the terrier barking in a frenzy below.

The claws of a fox leave in the mud the slenderest of lines, or tiny rounded dimples where they pierced the surface. The claws of a terrier are plain to see, and the farm cat left no trace at all of her sheathed claws.

Down the woodland ride, walking in the rut of the waggon wheel, the badger has been night after night. Beetles and slugs and worms were in the rut as he came; for he too has been to the hen-roosts, but only to pick up the spilled grain he loves or to lick out the feed bowl lying in the grass. The great badger that could bite a chicken in halves with one bite, prefers the taste of chicken mash to their flesh.

His tracks are clear in the ride; five-toed, with five long claws, and the great pad of the foot. But no one sees, or reads who has been to the coops.

In the gap by the hedge, the deer have been through to feed in the farmer's fields; the hedgehog has left prints in the ditch below.

The rabbits sit with lifted ears to listen. In the sandy soil at the mouth of the burrow the long hind foot leaves its impress, with the forepaws, close-placed.

In the straw-littered yard where they root for food, the pigs with rounded cloven hoof have cut the black earth. Through gateways into the high pastures flock the sheep, and their cleft hoof cuts the hard turf.

No one cares to read, even to notice. Only where cattle have been night and morning and churned up the mud they helped to make till the field gate is impassable, do we stop to consider.

Bird prints are there too. The green woodpecker stands on the soft mound of the red ant citadel, made smooth by rain; and there his print is clear. The coot walks with flanged toes over the snow of the frozen lake. The pigeons strut under the oaks.

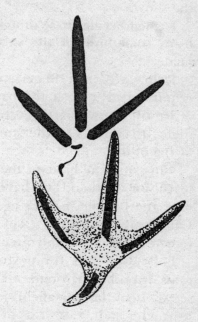

Tracks made by the same pheasant. Size ½. *Above*, In snow. *Below*, In deeper snow.

Everywhere there are prints to learn—trails of footprints for us to follow. From our knowledge of the habits of bird and animal we must determine the maker; what it was doing, whither it was bound.

Examine carefully, for each print has something to tell. The shallow impress, scarce to be seen, was made when ground and weather were dry. The spread print that seems too large for its maker, was made when the ground was too soft for a true record. The deep sand of the hill slope where the pheasant has walked on strong feet and dusted the fine particles through shuffled feathers; the mud softened after rain; the clay that many rains have moistened; all magnify the foot till we can hardly believe it was only the spaniel that came, or the blackbird that left so blurred and giant a foot in the snow.

Remembering these things, you may read more, and learn something of the weather since the mark was made.

Rain, with soft fingers, dulls its edge; frost will crumble it, slicing it through with microscopic plates of ice till no two particles touch. The thin frost of the night, that melts at the sun, has patterned it with a lacing of ice.

This, and the hour of the maker's coming you may learn, for wind and sun have dried the trail since. You may guess at the maker's age by the size of his prints. Often you may tell the sex of the animal, since male and female differ in size and often in detail.

Follow the trail. It must be there, even if in the short grass or on hard ground our unaccustomed eyes fail to see it. Look farther afield, for there is more yet to be learned from it.

Here are the slot of a buck, clear and firm, for the buck is in the pride of his life. The feet have 'registered'; the hind foot has fallen where the forefoot trod. The doe that followed has placed her hind feet a trifle wider, for she is broader in the haunch.

Look in the spring for the tiny slot of fawns that run after the does with uneven pace; now stepping far short, now stepping wide. For the fawn that soon will run fast as a dog, has to learn as any baby does, to go steady

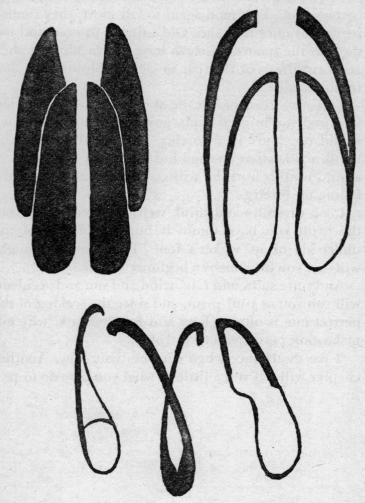

Footprints of fallow deer. Natural size. *Above*, Nearly registered. *Below*, On harder ground. Note distortion of forefoot on left.

and go straight.

As you may read the sign of youth in the wild, so age betrays itself. Feet tend again to fall short; they cannot register as once they did. Old injuries to hoof and toe show in the spoor; old claws have grown blunter, they are torn; the hoof that cut so clear is blunted too and round of edge.

You may read of the beast gone lame, for it has favoured the injured limb, going light upon it as we would do. Hurt in a foreleg, an animal chooses the uphill road, where strong hind limbs take the strain. If a hind limb is hurt, he will go down, with the weight falling on forelegs.

Look carefully and think well; and remember that the print you have found is but the picture of the underside of its maker's foot. That simple thought will save you from many a beginner's error.

And since snow and rain, wind and sun and accident, will rob you of your print, and since the seeking of the perfect one is often a long and fruitless task, why not make some permanent record of it?

Take the chance when it comes your way. Another chapter will tell you a little of what you may do to save it.

CHAPTER NINE

FINDING THE TRACKS

Foot and Food

In the field beyond the second hedge lies a shallow lake. Rushes grow in the mud at its edge; the mud grows wider as the summer heats come on, but the lake has never been known to dry.

There, in the long hours after school, boys come to fish and to bathe, and the fields are full of their laughter. But by day the lake is given to the wild birds and the creatures of hedge and field.

The grey rat creeps down, fearful of hawk and the javelin beak of heron. Through the rushes he goes to the water's edge and drinks with haste. Once at least in every twenty-four hours he must come, for he is a thirsty animal and could not live two days without water. Now as he drinks, his beady eye is on a silver form, lying on its side in half-mud, half-water, but breathing still with mouth and gills opening in gentle rhythm. The young bream, stranded by the drying of the water in his channel, lies waiting for the rains to come. But the rat has other ideas; and coming later, we shall find only bones and silver scales.

There is nothing the rat will not eat. Concrete and iron are not too hard for him to file, the face of his own brother thrown dead from the trap is not too awful for

Trail of brown or grey
rat in mud. Natural size.

him to mutilate.

The mud is starred with hand-like trails where he has run to forage. The ice-cream paper screwed into a ball and thrown away, his nose discovers; and he nibbles into its heart for the sake of the sweetness left.

Bait dropped by a boy as he fished lies in the water's edge. The rat picks it out and devours with relish the sour bread paste.

Follow the rat and you will come to see why he is detested so. Read the havoc he commits in barn and in bush, in the corn and among the nestling brood, and you will know why the bird in the hedge, seeing him sneak along the bank, warns all the wild.

But he has gone suddenly and in haste from the pond, for here are the tracks of his bounding; hind feet covering the fore, and the tail falling alternately to left and to right to leave a groove in the mud.

He went as the weasel came. He too with keen eyes was seeking fish. Last time it was roach. All day a fisherman had sat on the bank in a tranquil dream watching his float lifted on the nose of roach that wanted his bait but were too wily to take it. And then in the dusk as they rose and made rings on the still lake, the fisherman struck and foul-hooked a fish. But it dived and broke away, and the weasel found it lying on the mud with the bright metal of the hook still embedded in its gill.

The weasel comes to the fish the rat has devoured, and leaves his narrow prints beside the broad ones of the rat. It is strange how the weasel tribe loves fish. Stoat and badger devour it greedily, and the lithe otter has taken to a water life in order to obtain it.

But as he runs over the mud, there come one of

whom even the weasel needs beware. Twisting and diving in steep turns he drops, to alight beyond the mud in the shallows. There he draws up one leg and stands without moving, watching with an eye that has no expression, the shoal of minnows draw near to drift by that one green leg.

In the sandy grit of the shallows are more prints of the heron's toes, for this is his favoured spot. Even in winter, when the full lake is fringed with grey ice, he comes; to stand on its edge and wait for rat to flurry out, or a fish to slide from the shadow of the ice.

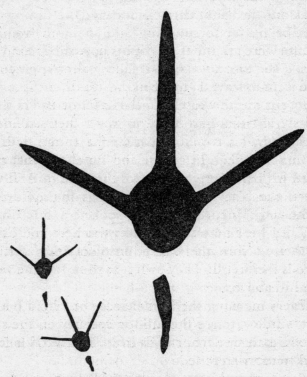

Prints of heron in river mud. Size $\frac{3}{4}$.

On the mud-bank there are castings of past meals; bleached bones among the shining scales of fish and the skull of a water-vole. For the heron, which eats the cannibal eel, the terror of the lake, eats amphibians too, and the mammals that come within reach of neck and bill.

Now at his coming, that fat-cheeked vole leaves her nibbling of green stems and dives to swim to the underwater entrance of her home.

More birds than the heron come; more birds than you have ever seen drink. The sparrow-hawk comes, for through the swelter of the day she has lain with open beak and wings outstretched above the downy young. The bright jay comes down, fresh from the killing of a mouse whose skin lies on the bank, turned neatly inside out. The pigeon walks like a lady over the green sward and dips her beak to drink where there is no mud. There come the squirrels that cannot eat if they are thirsty, and that like the purest water they can find.

All day, all round the lake, the thirsty ones creep down to drink. The mouse and the shrew that star the mud with tiny prints; the fox that laps with lifted ear alert; the blackbird and finch and the agile tits; all come and drink.

They were here and the lake was here and belonged to them, before man walked into his fields to till. The lake is theirs still. They own it as they own the wood on the hill above.

Every morning the farmer looks out from his breakfast window, to see the hill-top spinney on the sky. He knows each tree that stands in it. The wood is friendly and comforting to see.

But bird and beast that live in the wood, have never

owned man's right to be there. They were there before man's coming, for the wood is half-planted and half-wild.

There the kestrel breeds, and in the grass lie small grey pellets of broken beetle, and mouse bones. In the spring, when the downy young are in the nest, you may find legs of small birds caught to feed them. But the kestrel is friend to the farmer, who watches her hang with wings winnowing over his outlying coops, and knows she catches mice, for he has never lost a chick.

Rabbits are still in the spinney, as they were when the wood was wild. At dusk and at dawning they go down into the farmer's root-field; to scud back for the thicket as they hear the old black Labrador come labouring up the furrow.

Into the mouth of their burrows horse-chestnuts have rolled, and the rabbits have nibbled them, as they will when they come upon them in the winter days. There are the prints of rabbit claws in the loose soil, where they dashed in hurriedly.

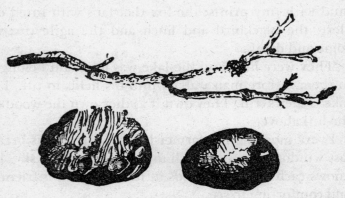

Ash twig from tree blown down in summer gale, nibbled by rabbits; potatoes gnawn by rabbits. (Essex)

And beyond them, with a den secure in the heart of an immense thicket of bushes and brambles, lives the cause of their hurry—the red fox that nightly steals down to the farm in hope of duck or chicken.

The mole tunnels under the scant grass, lifting a rough ridge to tell of his going. The vole in the bank, the mouse under the log, all these too are there as they were before man came. The wood, like the lake, belongs to them, and always will, for no man would wish to see it empty. And since man has made paths from wood to field for his own convenience, go down by the path to the valley and, keeping a watchful eye, you will find that man is not the only user. Birds both large and small come to gather the grit that lies in the gizzard and helps to grind the food.

Here is the soft body-feather of a pheasant, with the after-shaft growing from its base like a second, smaller, feather. In the wheat beside the path lie the feathers of partridge, tough and spring-curved, like the wing of the bird itself.

About the dusty surface where the nailed boots of labourers have loosened the earth, the hedgehog has zigzagged after beetles in the night. The mole leaves the press of his great hands upon it. The hare has loped by, seeming not to hurry but rather to linger in the confidence of her power.

The black feet of a magpie have left a trail to show where he hopped to pick the grasshoppers from the wheat edge. And here that rascal fox has been on his way back from the farm. Many a mouse and young rabbit he surprises in the wheat; deeds soon forgotten when the farmer comes to take toll of his ducks on their pool.

Trail of young hedgehog; thumb does not
show. Natural size.

Everywhere the birds and creatures move and feed, and leave the tale of their doings. Lake and spinney and lane, they all belong to them.

But how shall you read these tales so lightly written in the shifting dust, the mud that a single shower may smooth again? They are not always easily read; but the things most worth-while are not always the easiest to do.

I have made many a plaster record of a footprint, only to discover later that more prints had been recorded than I had known were there.

If you would see prints as the plaster finds them, then go if you can, with the sun in your eyes. Go when the shadows lie long across the fields, and the light is level in your face. There, then, are the tracks, bright with the end of day, and each black-edged with shadow.

But the best time of all is after dark. You will want a torch—not to find your way for torches are useless for that—but one with battery nearly worn-out, to see your prints. Hold the torch low, and level with the ground, and there they are; the weasel's at the base of his tree, where among the roots his lair is hidden, the badger's on his trodden path, the fox's round the log where he dug out the violet ground-beetle that was hunting for caterpillars.

They are all there. And there is no time, no place but some creature has been abroad in it. Find their tracks, and follow their trails; the more you learn, the nearer you come to knowing the animals in the flesh.

But before you do that, why not, as I suggested, make a record of the finds that thrill you most?

CHAPTER TEN

PLASTER CASTS

I believe that the best and the easiest way for you to make a record of a print you wish to remember permanently, and to be able to show to your friends, is to make a plaster cast of it.

When first I started, I carried with me all the apparatus I thought might be wanted during the day: strips of card to put round the print, to stop the liquid plaster running; a tin of vaseline to make sure the card came away freely from the plaster when all was dry; a mixing bowl and a spoon for making up the mixture; a tin of powdered alum, to ensure a quick smooth set; a bottle of water, in case there was none to be found when I wanted it most; old newspapers to wrap up the finished casts for taking home; and lastly, the plaster of Paris itself, often seven pounds of it, for I made thick casts in the hope that they would break less easily.

On many days I made no cast at all; there was nothing I found worth my taking. I came to grudge the weight at my back, and as time passed I found it was quite unnecessary.

I bought dental plaster from an oilman's for a few pence a pound more than I had paid for the other.

A few pence, for what a difference!

The dental plaster was superfine. It was dazzlingly white. It set quickly and smoothly and strongly.

I left at home the powdered alum and even the vaseline, for I found the card came off cleanly without it. Nowadays, you may obtain plastic strips that are even better than card, and that may be used over and over again without ever sticking or becoming roughened as cardboard tends to do.

I still must take my mixing bowl and spoon, my strips, and the paper clips that hold them in position and yet allow me to adjust them for size. I still must have plaster, but much less, for I know its strength when made up.

Off you go, then, all set to make the perfect cast. But what is the perfect cast?

If I were to tell you what I think are often the most interesting because they have character and a tale to tell, and if you were to go out and make a collection of such things, your friends would say 'What on earth did you waste your time taking those things for?'

For they want to see the perfect print; the one that really looks like the underside of a rabbit's foot (a hard one to get), or that really looks like the deer slot they expect to see. And that I expect, is what you yourself want.

But the perfect print, as I have said before, is hard to come by. You cannot make one. The leaf trodden under a toe has nothing underneath but the impress of itself. As the print is, it has character. Take away the leaf and you take away that character.

An animal slips, as animals do in the wet. Claws drag, and dig deep, seeking a grip. That print too, has character. But you would not want it for your collection. No one but you would appreciate it, or even understand it.

So, find the perfect print; the one without any ab-normalities whatever.

Walk beside the trail you have discovered. Examine with a keen and critical eye. By every likely-looking print plant a twig, so that you may find it again on your return.

I said, you noticed, 'walk beside your trail' not 'upon' it. And if that sounds so obvious as to be absurd, I can only tell you that I have been out with many children and with grown-ups, too, and most of them forget just what I have said; until they come back to have a second look—and find nothing but their own footprints.

When you have found all you want, or all you have time and plaster for, walk back, and search with double watchfulness. The tiny twig trodden in below a pad; that has spoiled a good print. The dead grass stalk fallen across the path and embedded in another print; that is a failure. The stone whose smooth bulge stands where the imprint of the ball of the foot should have been; that makes another to reject.

You will know it, when you come across the one you want, clean-edged and sharp and clear. Ring it round with card or plastic strip—now—before you lose it.

Make the card big enough to slip right round the 'mould'—that is, the print—without danger of pushing it out of shape, and yet without leaving too much space to be filled with wasted plaster. Press the ring gently into the earth and all is ready.

Go on, and ring every print you need. Or, if the card runs short, leave the stick standing, and remove the others to avoid confusion.

Now get your mixing bowl and spoon. Take the same bowl and the same spoon every time; you will get to know the quantities required for the work in hand. Mix the plaster well with water—but quickly—until it pours not too thinly, but not so thickly that it cannot find the tiny marks of claws you want to show. Add more liquid paste to the top of the first if you think it necessary; it will seal without a mark.

Now leave the cast while you make the others; give it ten minutes to set. Then take it up with the soil still sticking to it. Unless the soil peels off easily, leave it there. Put the whole cast into newspaper—back to back, if you are putting more than one.

Take it home without examination. And there, be patient. Place the cast under running water, and gently ease off the mud. Brush it if you must, but use an old soft brush; and remember that every stroke you make with it, rubs some portion of your cast away. It is easy to dull the edges of a good cast and spoil it after all your trouble.

Are you going to colour it, or leave it white? I hope white.

Remember to write on the back—in pencil—the name of the 'maker', the date, and where it was found. Sometimes it is useful to hang up your collection; then put in a loop of tape before adding the last paste.

And take care of your casts. Others may learn much from them—perhaps even the joy that can be got from simple pleasures.

CHAPTER ELEVEN

RECORDS WITHOUT PLASTER

There may be times, and I have known them, when it is impossible to obtain plaster or when you feel you would rather not carry its weight around with you.

You may still make records of the prints you see.

Remember your field note-book. You can always draw, for the model is there before you. It takes no more trouble to draw it than is needed to observe accurately—accurate observation is half the secret of success in any drawing.

But there are times when there is no trail of prints to follow; no spoor to examine. Then you must make the animal record its own comings and goings.

Make mud! Pour water gently and evenly over the chosen spot where you think the creature walks. Place paper beyond the mud and wedge it down with twigs pushed through or with stones at its corners. Use stout paper. It may lie for many hours; it may be rained upon; the dews will soak and soften it. And then instead of prints, if it is thin paper, there will be holes.

Remember—every touch of your fingers on paper, twig or stone, will be read by the animal you hope will walk over the paper.

I have used the mud method successfully for proving that badgers that climbed out of a deep pool in a stream, came in at the shallow end, and so must have

'Use your note-book'
Foxes and fox-cubs; sketches done from life. (Epping Forest)

used the deep water deliberately; in fact, they swam.

But mud dries quickly; and often you must find something that stays moist for longer. Then you must use the soot-and-oil mixture. This was a hint I read of long ago in a book by H. Mortimer Batten, and a very good one it is, provided that you are careful not to smear too much of the mixture for the animal to walk on to—and have to clean off, after.

Place the soot and oil on a board or card or thick paper. Pin it to the top of a fence post where the squirrel lands before running along the gate top. Place the clean paper beside it, and be sure you are nowhere in sight when the squirrel makes his leap.

Or place the sooty paper in the runway of a rabbit, where the mark shows he lands from the bound; and the clean paper on the next mark.—Fasten them with string round the trunk of the oak in whose hollow top the stoat has her hidden young; or on the bough where the squirrel runs from his drey.

These methods of oil-and-soot, and of mud, are easy to use, and simple in result if you can be sure of coming again before the paper has become a maze of trails that no one could unravel. (Such as the trails you might get, of rat and of mouse and vole.)

And one last word; the paper, the very taint of your touch, may be sufficient to drive away the creature you wish to come to know. Better no record at all, than to scare away a creature from its rights.

CHAPTER TWELVE

YOUR FIELD NOTE-BOOK

I started writing this book in a month of August when the swallows were gathering in hundreds about the Kentish farms where I stayed. The first week of August, I thought, and summer is done.

Yes, done indeed; and why should I be surprised? I could hear the harvesters purring up and down the fields; the grain was full and ripe, the straw bales grew in their scores about the stubble acres.

I watched the haulms of broad beans being eaten up and shot forth again. 'Clank!' went the binder, and gulped out a bundle of tied haulms. 'Clank!' 'Clank!' all day in the sunny hours, while I wrote with pad on knee.

This was a part of the mighty rhythm of the seasons, that brings a harvest every year.

Had my mind not been on this book, I would have written of the labour of the fields, that seems so happy and so slow and easeful, and that yet is so full of skill and the hardest toil. But I had no time to give. I made no note of the impressions of the moment as they fled.

And now I cannot write of the summer for the whole mood of the world is changed. Insects still hum among the trees. Swallows—though not the birds I saw—are about the barns.

But I have seen the great queen bumble-bee rise

from the bramble sprays above her home and, with a drone hanging over her abdomen ready for mating, sail off majestic and slow, up among the branches of the trees, to be lost in the blue of the sky.

At times, unable to sustain the flight, they fall to earth again and end their mating there; so that next spring the lonely queen may build her colony.

Now, in the sky by day and by night are the calls of redwings come to winter with us. Winter; it must be of winter that I make my notes, and keep them I will.

And you, if you are going to recall all that may happen in your hours afield, must keep your note-book too. Without it you can never remember all that you will wish.

What shall you put in your notes? First and always, the date, and then the place and the weather; for weather has a profound effect upon wild creatures as it has on us. Then, you will put in everything that interests you; all that seems to have point, everything that touches your imagination.

Make a note of it, there and then, at the time it happened. Nothing else will be so good, for nothing else can be really truthful. By being truthful, I mean that it records exactly what you saw or heard, no matter how far-fetched it may sound, or what you may have heard or read about it. To do that, you must use your note-book there, on the very spot.

There have been times when I enjoyed the writing of notes. But there have been many, many times, when I have had to force myself to write at all. Times when I could see no mark on the page but only the shadow of my pencil thickness. Times when I had to fight a weary brain to concentrate on the note that must go down, before I fell asleep again and forgot: nights so cold, I could not feel whether the pencil was in my fingers or not.

Yet I wrote the notes; and so will you. And from them, bit by bit, and piece by piece, you will come to build up a picture of the lives of those you watch. You will see the little incidents that make the daily round in the wild, as in our lives. You will come to glimpse the great underlying movements that make the rhythm of their lives; so that year by year song and nesting, mating, and the appearance of cubs, take place within the margin of a few days' difference.

Keep your field-books, and later, looking back through your notes and seeing them so fresh and true-to-life, you will be glad that you made them, and glad for the understanding they have given you.

For our minds are not like those of even the best-loved of the wild creatures. Ours are deeply enriched by thought and by remembering.

CHAPTER THIRTEEN

FOLLOWING THE TRAIL

The trail, in itself, is a line of footprints. But following it you may discover what an animal does, what sort of life it leads when it is neither moving to feed nor running from danger.

Its dwelling place; the arrangements it makes for its own comfort; the nurseries it builds; its play ground; the spot where it lies asleep in the sun. You may see all of these by following the trail.

The badger, greatest home-maker of them all, dwells in the sett his ancestors dug, for he can find no better spot. He alters and adds as every badger has done for a thousand years.

In the slope of the mound are his tunnels—hundreds of yards, a mile, of them—on different levels. There are the scores of entrances; some still open, some, long-lost doorways to forgotten passages. Not till some wanderer in the underground maze pushes one open from inside and clears away leaves and earth, can you guess they are there.

There are strange puzzles in the badger's life, that you perhaps, may help to solve. Near to many setts, there stands a tree, deep scarred by claws. Here, it is said, the badgers come to rear against the trunk, and measure with their claws their greatest height for the information of others.

But these trees are not at every earth. I have not found them in Epping Forest. Perhaps they are not needed there, for a Forest badger in a night of wandering may meet with all those he is likely to know in a lifetime.

It is possible that where badgers live, as on the moors, great distances apart, there may be some need, some use, for such a guide.

But the badger has a nose that tells him more than a dozen eyes; and on the trail he leaves, from glands beneath the tail, a drop of liquid; a scent upon the ground. The warm smell of it lingers long after, even to human nostrils. What then must it carry to the nose of a creature that lives in a world of scents that we never know?

Foxes and many animals do this, often in time of danger. I have been given the scent warning from a passing fox. It thrilled and stirred me uneasily; it meant fear. If it carried warning to me, what must it tell another fox?

But if the scratching-tree is not a message-post, what is it?

Some say that here claws are sharpened and cleaned.

But what need has a badger which will turn up more soil in a night than a man could, to sharpen claws? Or to clean them? I have watched badgers come home— and even after hours of rain, returning soaked and mud-splashed, they went straight underground. Any that cleaned claws on such a night would fill them again, descending his own tunnel.

I have seen scratching-trees—in Surrey—of the soft-barked elderberry; but no animal could measure its height on them for they were lying on the ground.

I have known badgers rear against trees, but they were finding through their noses whether I had left a food parcel in the tree. I have seen their claw scratches where they have dug away bark for the insects below. I have known them to come from the ground and stretch against a beech.

And that I believe is the explanation of these trees. They tell no more to passers than your cat conveys by clawing the leg of the table. Badgers are stretching there; as you stretch on first awaking; as your dog stretches rising from before the fire.

Then there is the puzzle of the bedding. Some watchers declare that Brock brings out his stale bedding to air in the sun. I have seen cartloads of bedding left on earths, but never known it taken down again. There may be shortage of bedding that makes Brock careful in other places. That still does not explain the bundles of new bedding that are so often left—and never claimed.

Why should an animal go a hundred yards down into the bracken and there bite off fronds, bundle them, clasp them beneath his body, and shuffle backwards with them on two legs, only to leave them lying on the floor of the wood?

I used to think my coming or a move of mine had startled him; that he had dropped in haste. But now I know the bundles are dropped in waste. I have gathered them, summer and winter. Our badgers, that waste so lavishly, certainly have no need to bring bedding out to air.

And what of the tales of badger and fox—this smelly neighbour that often takes lodgings in the mansion of the badgers?

People say that the stench becomes unbearable, that the badger at length clears out both fox and fox belongings. But I have sat many a time where I could hardly bear to be because of fox, and the badgers seemed to bear it calmly.

In 1948, a vixen had her cubs just below the badger den I watched. What with scent of vixen and the smell of the cubs in the earth and the stink of decaying bird and animal left around, I longed to go. Only the joy of watching made me stay—and the knowledge that the going of the vixen, always half an hour before the badger, was a test of how well I was hidden.

In the summer, the vixen left; and the badgers did not clear her den till 1951. Thus it comes that a farmer, visiting the earths one day, finds the leg of his prize rooster, with the celluloid ring still intact, lying outside the earths where badgers are; and blames the badger. How is he to know that fox it was that took it there?

But fox will clear badger too, for he wants none of the bedding left behind in the sleeping chamber. Out it all comes, to leave a clean slope of earth and nothing within. He drags deep grooves along which to clear the litter. But still there is left a ridge at the entrance to his den. That seems typical of the fox—a well-swept floor but a doorway piled with débris.

By that you may know his dwelling from the badger's, even though they be in the same sett; for the badger with great sweeps clears everything from the entrance and scatters it far and wide, to overspill the mound and roll below. There in the fallen earth I have found skulls of badgers long since dead, and the jaws of pigs that once were turned to forage on beech-mast and acorns.

But the fox takes many a den besides the badger hole. A rabbit stop will do, where in the single tunnel the young were born and covered in by day; for the fox can dig and dig well, and soon has it deepened and enlarged. The hole under the oak, where the grey squirrel hid at his coming; the gape torn in the earth by a tree uprooted in a summer gale; the hollow under overhanging roots—anywhere will serve, so long at it is dry and secure. Peer within at the torn roots that he sliced through as you would eat a carrot. What are roots to teeth that can cut strong wire mesh when poultry sleep on the farther side?

Look at his prints, where he had to straddle to get in. Not a single line now, but double; for he went in as your cat goes under a gate, as a dog squeezes under a fence.

So too in deep snow, when the fox bounds from you, you will find the hind legs thrown wider than the fore, to make a trail like a dog's.

But the fox is not the only adaptor of holes to its needs.

The squirrel fills a deep cavity with leaves to make a nursery. The nuthatch plasters with mud the fault in a branch or the deserted woodpecker home she has chosen for her own, and uses it year by year, leaving each spring just sufficient space for the passage of her body.

The great titmouse finds a cleft in the trunk of a tree and fills it with fibre and hairs, moss and feathers, till it is the depth she desires.

And those that must make their homes, construct to the right size and the right shape for their own bodies. Why should they do anything else? Woodpeckers drill holes in the stiff wood of trees. Sand martins with their

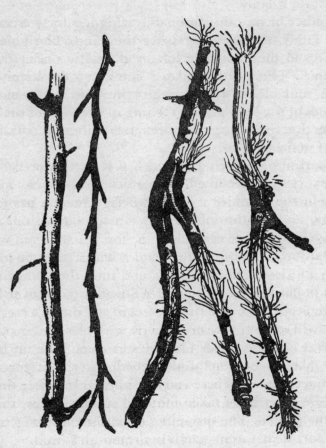

Damage by red and grey squirrels. (Epping Forest)

tiny bills, peck out tunnels in the hard sand and the chalk of quarry sides. Rabbits excavate a maze in the gravel bank. All their homes are made to measure—to fit their body.

Other birds, other animals, caring less for secrecy or for safety, use whatever space they find. The blue tit comes to the knot hole left by the falling of a rotten branch. The jackdaw takes a cranny on the limestone cliff, and fills it with sticks; or he finds a gap in the stones of the sea wall, an opening in the spire of the village church, a space between two chimney pots, the split in the trunk of a beech.

Starlings lay their blue eggs, pale as winter sky, in every hole unoccupied. The stockdove comes to the gap in the trunk of a beech where a branch has torn away, and on the soft brown touchwood within, she lays her two white eggs.

The mallard quits the pond where last spring the grey rat devoured her brood, and lines the hollow top of a pollard with brown and yellow down, to cover her fifteen eggs. The cole tit squeezes in and out of a crevice that will scarcely take my finger.

And not only birds use holes in trees. The noctule bat takes possession of the woodpecker nest for his summer retreat. Where you find one bat in a hole there will be other holes taken too; and you may know them by their smell. The droppings of bats smell strong; and the noctule has scent glands in the mouth as well.

Other bats are in the trees; the long-eared finds a piece of bark loose on an oak and hangs up behind it, with ears down-folded. Disturb his rest, unawares, and he flies with unerring aim through the bright sun to another tree.

The long-tailed field-mouse excavates a thumb-hole at the base of a tree, or in the ivy cover of a bank. Later comes the weasel and slips in, to find the trembling mouse at the tunnel's end. For even a hole may not be safety.

The red squirrel, flattened to a branch, sidles to the hole where the starlings have laid, and for all their fury and the blind courage of their dives, sneaks in and steals an egg.

But all the life of animals is not building home or nursery, essential though they be.

Here in the grass on the mound where fox and badger and rabbit live as neighbours, is a flattened space. It is not humans that have been picnicking this time, for there is no litter here.

This is where cubs have come in the warmth of the sun to romp and to gambol. Their future life they may largely live by night, but to fox and to badger cubs the sun is precious, as to us all. This is their playground, hidden from the sight of others.

Not only cubs, grown animals too that man imagines sleep through the day in dark tunnels, are often abroad in the sun. The dog fox curls in the crown of the pollard. The rabbit creeps through the brier to lie out of the wind. The vole dozes in the lee of a bush.

The smoothed hollow in the grass at the fringe of the thicket was not made there for nothing; and creeping up or watching with glasses from afar, you may see the sleeper in the sun, for these are the sunning spots.

And as they come to sleep in the sun, so the wild animals have their times of play, their ancient playing grounds, and the games that are their own.

The young rabbit is in the field, racing and leaping

while the older ones keep watch with ear and nose. He learns to sit on hind legs and box; he discovers the strength of those hind legs, whose kick may one day save him from the weasel. He listens for the warning thump at danger, he learns to give it and to act upon it.

In the home tree, the red squirrel family runs a breakneck race, down the bole and up, and out to neighbouring trees. Down and up they go, spiralling. They must leap where mother leads. They must follow or be bitten in punishment. Mad seem their games and reckless of the danger, but mother has the care of all at heart. Now she comes down to the straggler, the weakling of the brood. She comes to kiss noses, and encourage it to clamber after.

Where the squirrels sleep at dusk the red fox comes to play. Cubs pounce on beetles in the leaves; they race and tug and tumble. They come to the time-honoured play-tree where generations of cubs have played. They climb, and leap down upon brother or sister in the grass; they roll together snapping and biting.

And here, some time between dusk and dawn, they are brought their playthings; rabbit heads and legs, and wing of chicken. You may find their playthings as they left them at the end of play, lying scattered and forgotten.

Badger cubs play too, romping with the boar and sow. They know the play-tree, and on it you may find their flattened hairs, black-banded. And on the very crown of the tree are the hairs of grown badgers, climbed there to watch or hide, or perhaps to avoid the rough and tumble.

And wherever animals have been, on the trail or feeding quietly unobserved or at play, there you will find their droppings, or at least their latrines.

On the mound the badger digs his pits, changing them every few nights. His neighbour fox that will use his own doorstep, in the open chooses logs and stumps, or a boulder. There you will find his grey droppings, drawn-out with feather or bone projecting, and bright with beetle pieces. Look where the cubs were at play and you will find their droppings, made entirely of beetle remains.

The squirrel drops spindle-shaped droppings on logs. But he is so active you may look long without seeing any, for he scatters them as he goes.

Mice and rats make similar droppings, according to their size, and so do voles. The brown field-vole makes a clearing in his runway and comes there regularly until cleanliness demands a move.

Deer make droppings where they feed and often spill them as they run; dark and shining on the leaves. The little brown pellets of rabbits you must know, for they are everywhere.

Birds must leave their droppings too. The bramble trail hanging loose from the rock, was brought in the seed by a blackbird that had feasted on berries.

The tiny rowan growing far from any other, was dropped as seed by the mistlethrush in flight. The hard stones of haws fall where redwing and songthrush feed together. The pigeon from the oak has left stains of purple from the dark ivy berries. The starling has coloured tree and ground with the juice of elderberries.

And here, below her holly roost, the brown owl has cast grey bundles of fur and bones and beetle; the so-called pellets. Gather them and break them open. You will learn how the owl that eats so many beetles and mice and voles, varies his diet and kills blackbirds too, and casts their golden bills into the grass.

Many birds besides, cast the indigestible remains of meals; and all are worth investigation. Below the boulder where birds are plucked and eaten by the hawk; below the cliff nest of the kestrel, or the high perch of the peregrine; by the hole in the bank where a kingfisher has her tunnel nest; on the stones of the shore and the estuary flats where sea-birds rest; there you may look for them.

Pellets and droppings lie scattered everywhere on the earth. They will not lie indefinitely; for others besides you are interested in them.

The hedgehog comes in the night to the cowpat, for he knows there are beetles in it. He stands to sniff and leaves in the drying surface the imprint of his foot.

Under the pat are more beetles, and red worms and beetle grubs. Rooks know this, and the crow the farmer shoots, and the handsome magpie that he detests, and the little owl that eats the farmer's pests.

But the beetle is friend to us. The square-bodied dor beetle that knocked against you in the lane, was off to the field where all day horses have stood nose to tail under the hawthorns. He has gone to eat the droppings that they left. The three-horned typhoeus beetle trundles pellets from the rabbit mound, to be food for the grubs that will shortly hatch. With his 'horns' he manoeuvres them laboriously, to drop into the tunnel where the female waits. Dungflies swarm up in swift flight about your passing feet.

All these 'useless' insects are busy about their work of removing the droppings you would examine, and doing us the greatest service, for they sweeten and

Cowpat being buried by dung-beetles.

clean the surface of the earth for our use.

Have I said enough to show you that the trail has more to show than footprints, interesting though they are? That the way is full of interest and inquiry?

Then, as you draw near to its end, and the time comes when you may watch by day and by night, let me add a few words of advice.

The time will come when you wish to sleep out, when the last 'bus goes too early or the night and the moon make ideal watching.

There is no need for a tent. I have slept summer and winter without, and taken no harm. But I remember that damp rises to my warm body on even the driest ground at night. I remember the chill that strikes to my body before the dawn, and I take precautions.

I sit or lie with plenty below me; a good groundsheet first, and on top, all the clothing that is dry and that I can spare. I like a second thin groundsheet, to make a ridge-cover over me; and then, though it pour or the dew soak the grass, I am dry.

In bracken you may easily, with a handful of standing fronds, make a support to hold the string for the ridge of your 'tent'. If you sleep in a wood, then with dead and bent boughs you can make a frame for the cover that will yield and give to the night wind but will never break.

All you need is string, and that is something you should never be without. String, a penknife, and a shilling, the old saying said—and a very good one it was. To it I should add, matches. All these are things you can never know when you may want; they are part of the equipment you should have always ready, like the tape measure I carried, which weighed almost nothing and took almost no space at all. Over and over again I had to use it. Yet without it I should have had other measuring devices that you too carry with you. The size of my span from little finger to thumb tip; the length of my normal stride; the length of my shoe; the distance I can stretch with arms wide. You may not think these things essential now, but sooner or later you will want to use one.

One word more—on being lost. To me, it is like learning to ride a cycle; lose your pedals, but keep your head. Lose your way, but keep your head—be calm about it. Remember, that if you are really lost, and you have done as I suggested earlier, someone before long will come to find you.

There is much you can do, as you go, to avoid being lost.

Make a mental note as you come, of the position of sun or moon. Memorise the outline of the hills; the shape of tree masses. Look how the woods are placed on the sides of the hills, and against the sky on their crests. Mark the aspect of lonely trees that make a landmark—the fallen tree that lies alone; make a note in memory of the bridge you crossed, the waterfall you heard, the shepherd's hut you saw on the distant fell.

And remember to look back at times, and see what you will look for on your return. The turn of a head may make all the difference between recognition and being lost.

Go, with your young eyes, and your fresh mind that is eager for discovery. The world is full of wonder, and the world and the wonder lie at your door.

Why not open, and look out?

CHAPTER FOURTEEN

THE END OF THE TRAIL

The jackdaws mount from the steeple into the morning air and cry 'Jack-Juck!' 'Jack-a-jack-Juck!' to the golden sun.

The day begins; for you and for all the creatures that are awake in the light.

How often the world wakens with a song. The dawn chorus in the spring is such a joyous clamour that I cannot sleep but lie awake to hear. There is bird song, though, through much more of the year than this. I have lain all night on the cold October earth to see the dawn come in the east with such a gladness of the birds —robin, wren, hedgesparrow, pigeon and crow—it seemed impossible this could be the Autumn, till I looked again at the leaves where I lay, white-edged with frost.

If you would really know the beauty and the meaning of the new-found day, you must be out at its coming, lying in tent or under the open sky. The day may come cold and hard and grey, as many a day does. But life in the earth stirs at the warmth of the invisible sun, and the alarm clock of the wild we have spoken of, calls all to waken for the day's events.

The deer, the dun fallow deer of Epping Forest, stand under the trees against the growing light. Antlers move and drift across the arena with the gentle grace that belongs to the deer. I hear coughing; a rasping cough; a September sound—the challenge to come, to fight.

But there will be no fight, for the deer are moving off; going down into the bracken of the glade, where the first warmth of the sun will stay. The does are leading, intent on their work; the antlered bucks still face the east, and call. None has seen me, I may move without being seen. Without haste I gather my belongings; for I too will go down to the bracken by a path fringed with birches, and there I will watch.

I go quietly, steadily, without sudden move or any noise. I come as if I cared for nothing but the enjoyment of the moment, wrapped in my own happiness. I am happy; and I believe that is something wild creatures sense, just as you know the happy boy or girl without a word being spoken; for happiness is something we share.

But still I remember what we learned earlier, that until a creature wild or tame has really come to trust you, arms and hands are a symbol of danger and of hurt. I keep them still. I come as the hunter comes, whose tomorrow and whose whole future depend on his success.

I make no scrape of shoe on stone, no snap of twig: I move with scarce a rustle of leaf; content to give half-an-hour—an hour—of silent creeping, to see what I may hope to see. Every step I watch; I can never go too slowly. I put the heel down first, then feel with my toe for stone, for twig that may snap. You must never walk on your toes to move silently, for you are off balance. I balance at every step, never taking a pace longer than is comfortable.

So I come into the bracken, and the deer are there already, moving softly.

A doe comes to the path below me, and though I have made no move she lifts startled head and gazes where I stand. She lifts a slender foreleg and stamps; then, as if she has forgotten, looks away, reassured by my stillness.

And in that second I see a fox coming up the path from the stream. The doe has not seen, nor has he seen her, for he is tired, and brush and head hang low.

The doe turns, lifts her head—and now I know that she has seen, for she stands as all wild creatures can, without a muscle's move. She turns about and bounds into the glade, leaping past me where I stand.

The tail is lifted stiffly; I see the white rump streaks. The herd see too, for this is danger signal. They rise, they bound after, like a tide rising on a beach; they flee beside me, for the inborn fear of the fox is greater than the ingrained fear of man.

The fox has not altered pace nor lifted head; he comes on like a tired runner at the tapes, and so sees me at last. He swings aside with quickened step to go like a whirlwind over the leaves down to the stream again, to climb the next rise for home.

And as he goes, there comes, running fast, a collie trailing him with nose to ground; and behind her a small black mongrel, glad to leave all the scenting to her, if only he can keep up with the chase. But the fox for all he is so weary, will not let them lessen the distance that holds them apart, for he needs home, and peace.

There comes another morning, and I am out. The cuckoo calls, a hollow loveliness that no boy can ever imitate. Redstarts fly about the beeches and 'Whee-ut' incessantly.

There is a stream below; but more than the stream is rushing down that bed. A mallard duck rises steeply and goes over to the far bank and calls and quacks, imperious and anxious.

And now I see the cause of her anxiety. Over the bank edge comes a brown head, alert and eager; and following it the brown body of a stoat, and following his, that of his mate and then five young. In single file they come, curving and looping to pass out of sight round the bend of the stream. They have heard or seen me, and are gone.

But they will be back. For to this stretch came the mallard duck two days ago with all her brood, to let them taste their first water-delight; and now the stoat has found them out.

As I stand, I see the ducklings cross to the duck, going over the peninsula made by the loopings of the stream, to the mainland. Minute by minute they come from hiding and run through the grasses of the water's edge and over the dry leaves, to marshal behind her.

But they are doomed, every one. For tomorrow, today even, the stoats will return, and hunt them down; leap on them in the holes into which they have fallen; drag them from the logs under whose bulk they have squeezed for protection.

It is sad; but it is the law of life. The unwary, the unthinking, the unlucky in their birth, are caught. Perhaps the duck will nest again in another year, and remembering, lead her brood to safer waters.

These are tragedies; tragedy to the duck. There is nothing we can do to help them, and yet how often we add to them ourselves. Thousands of birds and animals are killed needlessly every year.

A fawn totters from the wood on to the road. The car is swift, the fawn is young. Before the driver has time to slow, the fawn lies dead in the road; and in the dusk a doe waits for a little one that will not answer.

A dog finds another fawn. It lies behind a beech, with long legs seemingly crumpled beneath it. It hears the dog coming; it trembles at his sniffing. Knock-kneed it rises, and runs towards the bracken where in the sun its mother sleeps.

The dog sees the big ears, the sunk body no bigger than a hare's. It cuts across the path of the fawn and, before the heads are lifted above the green bracken, the fawn is dead.

Now the deer come, buck and doe, swift and menacing. And the dog leaves his licking of the dead one's body and slinks off, for he fears the antlers of the buck and still more the sharp hooves of the doe.

These are tragedies that happen every year. But come another, happier time. Come so that none has heard or seen or smelled you. Lie in the bracken where the deer are.

Something—someone—has moved, close by. A fawn lifts inquiring eye and ear above the green fronds that are not tall enough to hide him when he stands. He looks without fear, for he has known nothing yet to make him afraid. He looks only in question.

But the doe is watching him, and she too lifts her head to see what he stares at so intently. Her eyes seek yours; you see them big with fear. Move no muscle, and the fear will go from the dark eyes; for the deer know as every animal knows, who is afraid and therefore foe, and also, who is friend.

But of all the times to become acquainted with wild life, dusk and dawn and the night that lies between are, I think, the best.

There is no chance to stand afar and watch. You must be there with them, as they move softly about you. It is the final test of your skill in remaining hidden. And still, it is possible to creep so that none shall be afraid. I have come when the badgers were abroad without sending them in; I have crept up while the fox was examining the logs on the earths, without his knowing I was there. I have hidden to watch him steal up, and rush away.

You must come and you must stand, so that no breath of you can reach the warning nose. You must be still; without a scrape of sleeve on bark, without the shifting of a foot; and then you will hear the walkers of the night moving quietly all around.

They rustle softly; they turn leaves with a roof in search of mast; they scrape noisily on the dry bark of logs where wood-lice are hidden and spiders; they move in the trees overhead, going by the paths they learned by day; they crawl in the grass beside you. Move a foot, and with sudden noise they leap away.

You can be there with them all, if only you will have the patience and learn the skill. But make one creature give one warning note and, like a pistol shot in the dark, it will start every runner off for home.

By many comings in the dusk you will learn the ways of the deer and the paths they take by night; as I can sit and see them now, miles away from them.

I see the great buck that had no right to the Forest, but had come from some Essex estate. I see him waiting dusk by dusk as I come to my watching; antlers above the bracken, watchful and still. He is there in the mornings gazing with untroubled eyes, for this is a beast that has no fear of man.

I hear him again as I heard him one Autumn night when I sat with feet in a badger earth, kicking in the leaves, crunching crisp acorns.

Suddenly, I hear his challenge; a roar, a threat in the dark. I hear him move; stealing softly close. He calls again, a few yards away, a sound that is savage and ugly.

Then silence, a long silence, while with ear and eye I strive to know what he is doing, where he is now.

Utter silence. Softly I get up and go over to a tree that has been an old friend, and climb into it. There I give challenge back, louder and louder; and he answers, bark for bark, roar for roar; until at last I call alone. Has he stolen away or is he still there, hidden in the night? I cannot tell.

I get down at last from my tree and go over to my watching. There comes no bark, no sudden rush. He has stolen away without a sound, hidden in a cloak of invisibility.

But I find I cannot rest on the ground, so I go over to my tree for the night. I am not afraid of him, for he would run at a shout. But I am unnerved, for no one of us likes to be startled, to be made afraid by a creature we had believed to be far away.

That is the fear the darkness brings. There *is* such a thing as being afraid in the dark. Feel no shame of it. Most of us have felt it when we have been alone in the night. I certainly have. There is nothing cowardly in it; it is our instinctive protection. It goes back to the days when our ancestors were afraid with good reason of beasts and of other men, by night. It was a good fear to have; for the man who was afraid and who took precautions, lived to see the dawn come through the trees.

Today, when the danger is gone and there is no need for us to fear any of our wild creatures, the fear remains. We must use it to teach us how to move as the wild creatures move, to know, without being known. People who have lived many years out-of-doors, with senses alert, quickened by the instinct of fear they have conquered, come to have an awareness so subtle and so keen, they can feel the presence of an animal without any reason for knowing it is there. This is the hunter's 'sixth sense'. They have made fear their servant, not master.

Now, as I go to my tree, I know the deer are friends for all that I have been perturbed.

I remember them as I have heard them in other nights; September nights, when with a whisper of leaves they come where I sit hidden in my tree. Half asleep, I hear their calls, the cries of fawn to doe, and fawn to fawn, like the baying of fairy hounds.

'Mah! Mih! Meh! Mih! Muh! Meh! Mah!' they call, and listening I can understand why those who dwell alone in woods and far hills can believe in beings we scoff at in the towns. For they hear sounds that we shall never hear; the voices of wild animals undisturbed, and the cries of birds that pass unseen.

I think of these things as I sit in my tree, with the squirrel feeding over-head.

The wind comes, it makes music in the leaf floor. It lifts the leaves till they over-run each other; leaf over leaf, thousands upon thousands of leaves running all towards me, with the sound of a tide on distant shingle. The tree moves behind me, like the great muscles of a back on which I lean.

And, into the sound of the wind's making, there comes another, closer sound; the deer are passing before my tree. A fawn eyes the tree curiously; my foot is hanging below the groundsheet that keeps the wind from my body. She steps over daintily, and sniffs without fear, then turns to rejoin the herd without haste. She knows that I am there, she is content.

I come again when the autumn sun has picked the leaves from the beeches, to see the white-faced badger steal into the mouth of her den.

I see her with her mate, drag home leaves from the rustling carpet. They make little lanes where they drag, till the den is ringed round with narrow tracks like the spokes of a cart-wheel.

I come still later when winter brings the hours of cold and hunger. While you sit in the warm room for tea, and the fire is bright, I am already out.

It is dark, though early still, but not as dark as many a summer night, for the trees are bare tracery on the sky, and the sky itself reflects the glow from big towns far away.

The earth is very still, without a move; there will be frost tonight. My fingertips are numb with cold, and everything I touch is chill.

I look back, where in the western sky the new moon, with a star in her heart, hangs white for frost.

I go to my tree, for tonight I shall hear the foxes run. And in the dark after the moon has gone down, I hear them, hunting, and calling one to the other through the still Forest.

'Yapp-yapp!' they cry, 'Yapp-yapp!' A hateful and monotonous sound. I follow their paths by the cries; and so in the night I hear them come, and pass, running on leaves brittle as broken glass with rime.

I tighten the belt that I have put on over all my clothing; for that belt holds off the arm that frost would lay around my waist.

To the north the foxes go, running side by side for all the half-mile that separates them. Thin in the distance become their calls, and then return. 'Yapp-yapp!' 'Yapp!' 'Yapp-yarr!' A sound strangely disturbing and disagreeable. So all night they run and hunt, and call, till in the dawn I see them going home, effortless still and fresh.

And now it is winter indeed. I come in a time of January snow, when boys and girls are happy at New Year parties. The snow is swirling still, and the lower boles of trees are wrapped in it. I shall see if the badger comes tonight, as I have seen her come so often, to lift nose to the freezing wind and creep forth.

I sit with the snow driving into my face, till I am white as a snowman; but I leave it so, for the snow keeps out the wind as nothing else can. As I sit there, on my rucksack, the fox goes by, grey shadow in the snow that seems grey itself as it drifts on to me.

An hour of snow. I am white from head to foot. I begin to long for home, and wonder if I shall sit all night and no badger come. And then she comes. A flurry of snow and she is hidden. But I can dimly see her den, and no one has re-entered. She is out in the snow.

Half-an-hour I wait, so that I shall not startle her in my moving. The storm has blown away, and in the dim light of my torch I see the shallow depressions that are all the last snow has left of her prints. I follow, to learn whether she has gone off into the Forest or paid a family call to a neighbour earth. She has gone to the Forest by the badger path.

I have no need to wait longer; I have seen what I came to learn. The evening is still mine to enjoy.

And later, as I sit in tube train or bright room I see again, as in a dream, a grey badger creep out into the grey-white of the falling flakes and vanish into a world of white.

But the longest winter must pass, and I come again when the days grow long, and the woods are green, and the grass stands high enough to bend to the wind, and shine in the sun. The willow-warbler sings in the oaks; the nightingale is in the thickets; my friend the fox is abroad again by day—to satisfy the hunger of young cubs.

I come again in another evening, when under the beeches the bracken leans and strains towards the sun it cannot reach. I come before the robin has sung his goodnight to the world, or the redstarts pipe loud and plaintively about their nesting trees.

In a spear holly I hear a commotion, a din. Two jays are pouring out their hate above the head of a brown owl. For the owl, they know, kills jays and eats them. This one they have found sitting out before his time. This is their revenge, though the owl takes little heed. In two different years, I have heard jays cry the hunting call of the owl, and as he answered excitedly, they slipped across and mobbed him; sign of almost human cunning.

But now the dusk comes. The jays are still, the owls

come into their own and sing duets to the oncoming of night, a medley as haunting and as lovely as any by day. They draw to one another through the trees, as if drawn by those cries.

There is a rush in the bracken on the slope below. Another and another; and the fox cubs are out, to race and play and fight and tussle with old wing or bone.

They stop. They sit down; they gaze in a silence of wonder. For while they played, I have crept down through the bracken and over the lank grass. I have moved when no eye was turned in my direction, when no ear was listening. And there I sit, huddled in a coat, formless and shapeless; and the cubs stare, in-credulous. One moves to the back of my coat, and sniffs.

I sit without a move. He tears away over the earths, and in a second, all are gone. But not for long. In a moment they have forgotten and come to race again. Nearer and nearer they pass to where I squat un-moving. Perhaps another will venture to sniff.

But their play is nearly ended. The robin pipes, loud and wild and beautiful, her lament for the day. Shadows come to lie where no shadow was before; the trees take on such shapes as they never wear by day.

The owls have left their calling, and are hunting in the glade beyond where the last light seems to linger. There is a wariness in my being, a sensitiveness I share with the wild creatures. The light fades. The bracken is no longer fronds, but a dark mass without form. Only the whisper of feet tells me the cubs still play. Night is drawing curtains in the house of day.

Then, like a challenge of the night, out of the darkness comes a yell; another and another, terrible and strange.

As at the holding of a warning hand, there is silence. The whole night listens. Every fox cub is still; and I shall see them no more this night, for the badger has cried, and fox cubs creep to bed.

Still the night waits, for what may come; and there it is. Not a yell, but a whistling, trembling hiss that carries far and strangely through the night. And at that sound, a brown owl with a pair of downy young in a beech, shrieks her horror of all badgers; and pandemonium is loosed.

The badger yells and hisses. The owl shrieks louder with each sound, louder and higher, till the animal on the ground raises his in reply, and owl and badger mock and deride each other. Minute by minute, for twenty minutes they call. Till at last the badger wearying of it all and unable to stand any more, moves off, yelling still at intervals as if he would have last word. But the owl follows above, like a demon in the trees.

So I come, and the evenings are full of beauty and joy, and of the strange things we can only learn by being with their makers.

And when the badger is gone right away, to leave his prints in the sand of the Forest path; when the swallows have passed over high in the dark sky, and the nightjar is reeling his long 'jar', and I can keep awake no more, I creep over to where the blankets lie waiting ready, folded on the ground.

Thankfully I crawl in and keep eyes open for a while to see the stars hung overhead; I hear the night wind whispering, and to its voice I fall asleep: the sleep of the truly tired, the truly happy.

It is dawn before I open eyes; the dew hangs in

glistening points from each bracken tip.

But somebody is annoyed.

'Chuttah-Chutter-Chuttah!' I hear him exclaim.

I am in his way, such an obstacle as he has not encountered on the way home before.

'Chuttah-Chutter-Chuttah!' Preposterous, that such a thing could keep him from bed. And in a trice, he is in bed with me, running through. I lie still, fearful of moving and frightening him.

He comes to my foot and runs out, and sits a moment on my other toe. I know him well. He is the mouse that has a store of beech nuts in the oak, and a gnawn bone under the badger play tree. He is friend of mine. . . .

And now once more, and for the last time in this book, have I said enough, told you enough—and that is indeed little enough of all that might be told—to make you want to watch, to be patient and be proud to know the animals as your friends?

Then, let me tell you one last incident. True, as everything in the book is true.

I had been making friends with badgers for five months. Night after night I had come, no matter how tired I was, how bad the weather. I brought them food; onion-and-potato mash; some of my sandwiches now too stale to eat; eggs, bad and good; bacon rind and cheese rind; all the odds and ends that I could spare; and fish. Fish of all sorts and in all conditions. And they ate the lot. . . .

I come one night when the moon hangs bright and high, and the strange shine of her light on the ground fades and brightens although I can see no cloud. Hour by hour I wait expectant, for here at last is a time when

I can see all that takes place.

The hour of midnight strikes in a distant church tower and dies away over the Forest. Still I must not sleep, for the badger must surely come now. Then through half-opened eyes I see her; the sow that is to bear cubs within a week or two. She comes cautiously, without a sound. She creeps from the mouth of the den to stare at my offering of food, lying wrapped before her. Wrap it I must, so that if I fall asleep before they come, the badgers will waken me with the sound of their tearing.

The sow stretches her body long, till she looks the weasel that she is. She reaches out to the parcel, sniffs, and softly withdraws. I wait, for assuredly she will come again. Has she not come to expect the food, night by night? And she has no idea that I am there.

But the head that rises into the light of the moon is bigger, with broader bands of white—this is the boar. He turns without a sniff at the food, in my direction.

I see him jump, but on he comes, staring apparently at the thin groundsheet that I have thrown over my coat to keep out the night airs.

Very slowly he comes and, four inches away, stops and looks into my face.

The night hangs on a breath. My own breathing I cannot hear. One never holds breath to be silent, for at last it must burst out. Breathing falls naturally into a slow and gentle evenness of rise and fall. But the badger, surely, can hear the wild thump of my heart. For here is the test, the proof of friendship. We are face to face, each knowing that the other knows.

And then, without haste, the badger turns—and digs a hole next to the root on which I sit. I could put out

152

my hand, and pat his hard coat.

But I sit instead, with one of the shyest creatures in all our land, in trusting confidence beside me.

I may never know again, a badger out-of-doors, as tame as this. This is indeed to know, and be known. We are friends together.

CLASSIFICATION OF ANIMALS

Every known living thing has been placed with greater or less success into its place in either the Animal or the Vegetable Kingdom. It is generally easy enough to say into which Kingdom it should go; it is by no means always so easy to decide just where it belongs in that Kingdom. When we come to the simplest forms of life, we find that scientists have not been able to agree even to which Kingdom they belong. Zoologists, who study animals, claim them for their own; botanists, who study plant life, say they are plants.

How do scientists decide or try to decide these things? How do they set about placing the new species of plant and animal that are discovered each year?

To start with, and as a very simple guide, we may say that if a living organism can draw food from the minerals in the earth, then that organism is a plant, it belongs to the Vegetable Kingdom.

If on the other hand, it cannot feed on mineral salts but requires food that has been prepared as the body of plant or animal, then it belongs to the Animal Kingdom.

Plants, we may say, live on inorganic food: animals, on organic food, that once was part of the organs of some other living thing.

These are only simple rules, and simplified rules tend

to have exceptions, but remember them and you will not be often wrong.

Here is a simple classification of the Animal Kingdom, from the lowest to the highest, showing the Phyla or main divisions. A Phylum (Phyla is the plural) comes from a Greek word meaning 'race'. Into a Phylum go all the animals with a common ancestor, and that possess the main characters of the Phylum.

A Phylum is divided again into Classes, the Classes into Orders, the Orders into Families, the Families into Genera, and the Genera into Species.

Phylum, Class, Order, Family, Genus, Species.

Here, very simply, are the Phyla of the Animal Kingdom.

Protozoa (First-animals). Animals composed of a single cell, and living an independent existence even though joined in a mass, *e.g.*, Amoeba.

Porifera (Pore-bearing), *e.g.*, Sponges.

Coelenterata (Hollow-bodied), *e.g.*, Hydra.

Echinodermata (Spine-skinned), *e.g.*, Sea Urchin.

Bryozoa (Moss-animals), *e.g.*, Plumatella.

Vermes (Worms). Flat and Round Worms, *e.g.*, Liver Fluke and Hookworm.

Annelida (Ringed-worms), *e.g.*, Garden Worm.

Arthropoda (Joint-footed), *e.g.*, Crabs, Centipedes, and the vast host of the Insects.

Mollusca (Soft-bodied), usually have protecting shell, *e.g.*, Snail, Slug, Octopus.

Prochordata (Towards-backboned-animals), *not* the ancestors of Vertebrates, but possessing some of the characters that Vertebrate ancestors must have had. *e.g.*, Lamprey, Amphioxus.

Vertebrata (Animals-with-vertebrae, or backbone joints), *e.g.*, Fish, Bird, Man.

Since most of the references to animals in this book have been to vertebrate animals (you remember we agreed by 'animals' to mean 'Vertebrates') here are the Classes of the *Phylum Vertebrata*, with examples of species from the book.

Pisces (Fish), *e.g.*, Herring, Roach, Bream.
Amphibia (Both-lives). Animals that live first as fish and then become land animals breathing air as we do, *e.g.*, Newts, Frogs, Toads.
Reptilia (Creeping-animals), *e.g.*, Grass-Snake, Smooth Snake, Viper, Common Lizard, Sand Lizard, Slow-Worm.
Aves (Birds), *e.g.*, Sparrow-hawk, Moorhen.
Mammalia (Possessing-mammae, or milk-glands), *e.g.*, Stoat, Hedgehog, Man.

I want to say a word or two more on our mammals. None of them lays eggs (as the Duck-mole of Australia does, though it is a mammal). None of them carries its helpless young after birth, in a loose pouch outside the body (as the Kangaroo does, though it is a mammal). Ours belong to the highest kind of mammals.

Here are the mammals I have mentioned, in their Orders.